Also by T. E. Corner

List for Santa, List for Life!

Positive Thoughts, Positive Life!

Life Is Fine When You Are Aligned!

Mommy, Why Do You Have Two Birthdays?

Borrowed Eyes and Feet: Finding Enlightenment after Rage

Assholes to Angels: A Change of Mind in the Workplace (and the World)

What You Eat, What You Drink, What You Breathe, What You Think

Egoic Tendencies

NOW I LAY THEM DOWN TO REST

T.E. CORNER

Balboa Press books may be ordered through booksellers or by contacting:

Balboa Press
A Division of Hay House
1663 Liberty Drive
Bloomington, IN 47403
www.balboapress.com
844-682-1282

Print information available on the last page.

ISBN: 979-8-7652-4477-7 (sc)
ISBN: 979-8-7652-4476-0 (hc)
ISBN: 979-8-7652-4478-4 (e)

Library of Congress Control Number: 2023915561

Balboa Press rev. date: 11/13/2023

Contents

Egoic Tendencies

I Am Better Than All of You

Life Is Just a Dream

Sitting on the edge of his bed, Wayne leaned forward, placing his elbows upon his knees. He rested his face in the palms of his hands, giving himself a mini face massage. Rubbing his eyes and face with the tips of his fingers, he slowly ran his hands through his hair a couple times. He opened his eyes momentarily and closed them again, continuing the mini face massage. Rubbing his eyes in a circular motion, he slowly counted to himself. "One, two, three, four."

He moved his fingers to his forehead and then back to his eyes again. The pressure from his fingertips pressing upon his eyes seemed to cause bright flashes of light underneath his eyelids. The more he rubbed his eyes the more frequently the flashing occurred, followed by a glowing sensation. His fingers glided over his eyes once more before moving down his cheekbones toward his upper lip at the base of his nose. His hands slowly slid away from his face and came together in a prayer pose. His chin rested upon the V shape that was formed by his thumbs and forefingers. He propped his nose on the tips of his forefingers and middle fingers.

With his eyes closed, Wayne thought about the nursery rhyme, "Row, Row, Row Your Boat."

Row, row, row your boat,

Gently down the stream.

Merrily, merrily, merrily, merrily,

Life is but a dream.

He pondered the meaning of the nursery rhyme, having always been befuddled by the last line: "life is but a dream." He thought to himself, *What in the world does that mean? The English language is so strange. If I substitute "but" with the word "just," the entire meaning changes. Life is just a dream. Life is just a dream?*

He repeated the nursery rhyme:

Row, row, row your body,

Gently through your life.

Happily, happily, happily, happily,

Life is just a dream.

After several minutes of analyzing the meaning of the nursery rhyme, never coming to an exact conclusion, he began his evening reflection and meditation.

"Now I lay my egoic tendencies down to sleep, I pray the Lord my soul to keep. If my egoic tendencies should die before I wake, I pray the Lord my soul is awake.

"Spirit am I, a holy Son of God, free of all limits, safe and healed and whole, free to forgive, and free to save the world."[1] Wayne paused. Taking a breath, he began again. "I am not a body. I am free. For I am still as God created me."[2]

Wayne sat in silent reflection. A gentle breeze flowing through the branches of trees outside his bedroom window whispered in his ears. Thoughts flittered about his mind. *Although I cannot see the breeze, somehow it makes its way through the branches of the trees. It seems to make its way around the branches; but, in truth, it crashes into the branches.*

Watching the branches sway in the wind is beautiful, calm, and relaxing at first glance, but there is both force as well as resistance going on here. The breeze gains momentum and turns into a strong wind. The trees continue resisting the wind, swaying back and forth., sometimes violently. When the wind is strong enough, branches will crack and break, and maybe the tree will fall in a somewhat violent exchange.

Wayne enjoyed his evening practice of sitting quietly before bed to reflect and meditate. But on this night he was interrupted. He was not exactly sure why, but a loud ringing in his ears broke the silence of his evening ritual.

"Holy shit! I can't believe I never noticed this," he mumbled to himself. "It never stops." He bounced between expressing his thoughts out-loud and keeping them to himself.

Has it always been like this? Why am I noticing this now, when I'm finally comfortable sitting in silence? And it seems as though I won't be able to enjoy any real silence. I always had some noise in the background, music or other distraction, drowning out the ringing.

Now that I have finally become accustomed to sitting in silence, I can't ignore the noise. The more I pay attention to it, the louder it seems to be. And I can't turn it off. This sucks! But it does make sense, because this is what I always wanted. For practically my entire life, I was drowning out the world, listening to music with the volume turned up loud. When I studied, when I worked, when I exercised, and even when I went to bed. I asked for it, and now I am getting it. Interesting how things play out.

His wife, who was already fast asleep, was awakened by Wayne's murmurings. She asked, "Is everything OK?"

"Yeah, sorry," he said.

"Go to sleep, honey. It's late," she whispered as she rolled over onto her side to fall back to sleep.

"Soon. Love you," he whispered.

Sue fell fast asleep again, coughing up a slight snore every few minutes, sounding like a car engine sputtering. This made Wayne chuckle quietly to himself, trying not to be too loud and wake her again.

Wayne turned to grab the covers and pulled them back. He slid his feet under the covers and laid down on his back. Resting his head on the pillow, pulling the covers up to his chest, he stared up at the ceiling, reciting his affirmations a few more times. "Spirit am I, a holy Son of God, free of all limits, safe and healed and whole, free to forgive, and free to save the world. I am not a body. I am free. For I am still as God created me. Spirit am I, a holy Son of God, free of all limits, safe and healed and whole, free to forgive, and free to save the world.[1] Amen. I am not a body. I am free. For I am still as God created me."[2]

He turned on his favorite Peter Kater music and *om mani padme hum* Buddhist chant to play quietly in the background, but not too loudly to disturb his wife's sleep. His mind continued to race until he drifted off to sleep, slipping into the dream world.

The dream world always seemed so real. He had visited so many different places, and he had many different and exciting experiences. But he rarely recalled any of it upon waking. Could it be death was similar to waking from a deep sleep? Throughout our lives we experience so many things, visit so many places, and have many different experiences, just like in our dreams. But when we die and return to Source, it must be the same feeling we experience when waking from a night's sleep.

Upon waking from our dreams, we rarely recall any of them. At death all of our life experiences are forgotten but not lost. Although he could not remember the details of his dreams, there were always remnants of his dreams stored away in his consciousness. This must be what death is like. Especially since life is really just a dream.

He was drowning, held down by a tremendous weight which he could not see. He could not touch it, yet he could feel its burden. The weight felt like a few hundred pounds were on top of his head, preventing him from being able to lift it. He was unable to break free and could not look up to see the light.

"How is this even possible?" he asked himself. "There is nothing on my head. I know this weight does not exist! No one can see it. I cannot see it, but I feel it every waking moment."

He wanted to break free from this hell but could not escape it. He was a prisoner, and at the same time, he held the key to his freedom. "I am burdened by the demands of the world: work, taxes, money. And although they are blessings, marriage and family feel like tremendous weights preventing me from breaking free," Wayne spoke out loud.

He wanted to break free. He must break free in order to escape this egoic world. It never suited him.

"All of the things of this world seem to elude me. In particular, happiness and prosperity. Why? I understand the universe is abundant and free-flowing, yet I cannot seem to access it," Wayne continued to speak out loud.

His mind felt like it was under immense pressure, sort of like a tub filled to the top, or a dam holding back an enormous amount of water. The more water that accumulated, it created more pressure, which continued to build up. The only thing preventing the release of the pressure was a little plug in the drain. He wanted to pull the plug so he could release the pressure in his mind—all of the doubt, the fear, and the frustration.

"I know I have access to infinite intelligence, prosperity, and abundance. I can sense it but cannot access it! My mind feels like it has reached its capacity, but with all the wrong information. Nothing else can enter—nothing good. If I could just release the pressure from all of this anxiety, worry, doubt, and stress, I will be free! Could it be as simple as pulling a plug, like in a tub? Once the blockage is removed, everything is released."

Wayne stretched his right arm out in front of himself and upward toward the sky. He then reached his hand around the back of his head, he took a firm grasp of the chain that was attached to the plug and pulled as hard as possible! Like a dam holding back an ocean of water, all it took was one twig or stick to be removed, and all was released! This was Wayne's moment of release and freedom.

Once this task was carried out, meaning and attachment were no longer necessary. Who we believe ourselves to be, and what we become, are defined by the things of our world and what we fill our minds with. We accumulate what we believe to be knowledge, facts, and figures, but it just clouds our connection with Source. On top of that, we accumulate things and feel we must protect these things from theft and decay, which only fuels jealousy, envy, hatred, and war.

Welcome to the ego!

On the other side, infinite intelligence is available to all of us. The moment we realize infinite intelligence and awaken to higher consciousness, life as we know it changes. There is no price tag, there is no scarcity, there are no limits. Although the cost of this higher awareness is the loss of our egoic tendencies. It's not so bad, but it's also not so easy.

What prevents it from happening is attributable to our belief systems or, more accurately stated, our doubt systems. Our minds are impregnated with doubts and fears that are so strong and prevalent that they prevent nearly every human being on earth from achieving higher consciousness.

Unbeknownst to us, it is always present. Fueled by lie after lie and fear upon fear, it causes stress, anxiety, and doubt. Like the tub filling with water, our minds fill with egoic thoughts of fear, stress, anxiety, and hatred. The beauty of being human is the desire to seek a higher awareness, finding a way of pulling the plug to release the burden of resistance.

Not everyone pursues higher awareness, though. But those who do are aligned and powerful enough to elevate the consciousness of the entire planet—similar to what Jesus Christ, the Buddha, and Lord Krishna did, and still do to this day.

When we awaken to our fullest potential, we are aware of its presence everywhere and in everything, sort of like the ringing in Wayne's ears. Despite it always being present, he never noticed it because he had always drowned out the ringing by filling his ears and head with noise. But the moment he achieved pure silence, the ringing was so pronounced that silence was nearly impossible to experience.

The mind and the ego act in a similar fashion. We have been filled with doubt and resistant thoughts for practically our entire lives, yet we are completely unaware they exist. When we finally notice the self-defeating chatter in our minds, it is so overwhelming that it seems insurmountable.

This is a ploy of the ego. It does not want us to awaken and realize that all things are possible with God. It was Wayne's realization that all he had wanted was already there at his fingertips.

His difficulty in realizing it was simply because his expectations were on a larger scale. Everything he desired had been given to him all along, just not in the grand spectacle he had imagined. He simply did not realize it. He has loved and has been loved. He has healed himself and has seen others heal. He has lived a rewarding and prosperous life.

Despite it all being right there at his fingertips, he had fallen for the ego's allure of scarcity and fear. The ego wants us to have a scarcity mindset, believing there is not enough for everyone. Then our reality becomes an existence of defense, hurt, and attack in order to protect what we believe is ours.

What a sad existence. Although he had lived the scarcity lie, he could not seem to break the cycle. And there are two ways to accomplish this:

at death, when we return to Source, or by breaking through during this lifetime to achieve higher consciousness.

Our egoic tendencies honor all of the wrong things.

Opposite George

> "Offer your brother the gift of lilies, not the crown of thorns; the gift of love and not the "gift" of fear."[3]
>
> —*A Course in Miracles*

> "Between the banks of pain and pleasure the river of life flows."[4]
>
> —*Sri Nisargadatta Maharaj*

Stop Reminding Me

It was a Thursday afternoon when Wayne's phone rang. Wayne looked at his phone and saw the name of his good friend, Gary DeAngelis, flashing on the screen. *Why is he calling me on a Thursday?* Wayne wondered to himself because Gary usually called on Fridays.

Wayne tapped the green phone icon to answer the incoming call and quickly tapped the speaker icon to enable speaker mode. "Gary D! What's up?" He could hear Gary's voice coming from the phone sounding like he was far away, or like a tiny ant was speaking from inside the phone. "Hold on, I'm trying to switch to speakerphone," Wayne yelled into his phone.

Wayne tapped the speaker icon again, and Gary's voice came booming through the phone. "Wayne Renroc!" Gary said. "Thanks for picking up. It's been a while. I didn't know if you went rogue again."

"Nope! I'm still here, Gary."

"How are Sue and the girls? What's the latest with work?"

"She's doing well, and the girls are awesome. They're busy with school, softball, tennis, soccer, and lacrosse."

"Great to hear. You know, Wayne, I still worry about you," Gary said in a concerned tone. "I don't want you to go back to doing the things you did in the past. It worries me at times."

"Come on, Gary!" Wayne paused, frustrated by Gary's comment. "Dude, what are you worried about? That was a long time ago. It's not going to happen. And even if it did, it doesn't matter."

"Yes, it does, Wayne! It scared the shit out of me when we were in college, and I worry that you will go back down that path." Gary reiterated his concern.

"Gary, no offense, but you're an idiot. Why are you holding on to the past and what happened years ago? I'm fine. I don't even remember that crap anymore, until you bring it up. I wish people would leave me alone and stop reminding me."

"But I care, Wayne. You are such a big part of my life."

"Thanks, Gary, but you don't need to worry. I can't even imagine doing that shit again. It fucking hurt! I don't even know how I ever did it in the first place. Although I am glad I did. Because, at the time, it was a release for me."

"It hurts me to even think about it." Gary paused. "Maybe you did it to punish yourself."

"Yeah, good point. I'm sure that was a part of it. I probably took on the burden of my parents' divorce. I took on the shitty energy of my stepparents. I carried my parents' divorce and their issues as though they were mine, and I crucified myself for it. Pretty stupid. But it was a part of my journey, and you know, I always felt as though I was in control and would be OK. Sort of like the 'Footprints in the Sand' poem."

"Dude. You were not in control! Sorry, but you were pretty messed up and out of control!"

"Are you sure about that, Gary?"

"Heck yeah. I'm sure!"

"Sure, when I was blind drunk, I was completely out of control. I will give you that. But I am no longer that person. And even if I am, who cares?"

"I care!"

"The problem, Gary, is that in the eyes and minds of everyone else, I am still that person. And they hold that version of myself over my head, to remind me of what I once did and who I once was. It's like they are holding that person hostage and will never let it go. It's really ignorant and annoying." Wayne paused to catch his breath and take a sip of water. "You are such a great friend, Gary. But please stop! That's not who I am. I don't think about it at all until someone reminds me. How can anyone allow positive change to happen in their life when people always remind them of who they are, or who they once were?" Wayne asked.

"What do you mean?"

"I'm perfectly fine, until you decide to remind me of my past transgressions. That's why forgiveness is a farce. People might utter the words, 'I forgive you.' But it's a damn lie! Humans do not and cannot forgive, because we have the gift, or maybe it's a curse, of remembering. In order to forgive, we must forget or release. And since we cannot forget, therefore, we do not forgive. Spiritual teacher Ram Dass once said, "'If you think you're enlightened, go spend a week with your family.' Even when we change for the better, our family is always there to remind us of who we once were."

"OK. I'll do my best, Wayne. But I still worry."

"Thanks, Gary. That makes one of us. Eckhart Tolle wrote in his book, *The Power of Now*, 'I have little use for the past and rarely think about it.'"

"Who?"

"Eckhart Tolle, a spiritual teacher. When I bought his book several years ago, I was so excited to read it. I remember sitting in Starbucks when I pulled the book out of the plastic Barnes and Noble bag. The receipt clung to the cover as though it knew I would soon be finished with the book after reading those words on the first two pages.

Wayne repeated the sentence from Eckhart Tolle's book. "'I have little use for the past and rarely think about it.' Then I closed the book and put it back in the bag. I didn't need to read any further. I gazed out the window of the Starbucks for a few minutes, losing myself in what I had just read."

"So you never read the book?"

"Not really. I received his message loud and clear in those few words and felt no need to read any further. I received his teaching, which was so powerful! But, of course, I am constantly reminded of my past. Sometimes I want people to just leave me alone."

"I'm not going to do that, Wayne. You know that. You're my friend, and I am here for the long haul." Gary smiled.

"Thanks, Gary. You are the greatest friend a guy could ask for," Wayne said in sincerity. "Although I often wonder why you remained friends with me when I was such an asshole to you in college."

"Yeah, you were a dick at times. But we had fun together, and you were always there for me. That meant the world to me, and I am grateful for your loyalty and friendship."

Wayne and Gary continued talking for a while longer. Gary would always rattle Wayne's cage, testing and challenging him. He was always fascinated by Wayne's approach to life and his perspective of the world.

Opposite George

> "In the holy instant it is understood that the past is gone, and with its passing, the drive for vengeance has been uprooted and has disappeared. The stillness and the peace of now enfold you in perfect gentleness. Everything is gone except the truth."[5]
>
> —*A Course in Miracles*

Death of the Body. Birth of the Soul.

Sitting at the kitchen table, Wayne was lost in thought. *I want to hug her, but I am afraid. I see her body. It is frail. She is weak. I can't bear to see her in pain. I fear and loathe old age and death. I have been led astray once again, believing the lie that we die.*

He thought about the opening lines from *A Course in Miracles*: "Nothing real can be threatened. Nothing unreal exists. Herein lies the peace of God."[6] This also made him realize how far he was from truly grasping the Buddha's Four Noble Truths and the Eightfold Path.

Wayne's thoughts continued. *How can I not be attached to a loved one? Seeing her in her old age and struggling with pain and discomfort is heartbreaking.* He recited a line from *A Course in Miracles*: "I am not a body. I am free. For I am still as God created me."[7]

Grabbing his iPhone, with his right thumb he swiped the screen in an upward motion to view the open apps. Swiping the screen from right to left with his index finger, he scrolled through the open apps searching for the Safari browser. He tapped the icon to open the browser on his screen. In the bottom right-hand corner, he tapped the double squares to view the browser tabs. With his index finger he scrolled through the open tabs until he found the page for chapter 16: VI in *A Course in Miracles* and began to read to himself.

> For you will realize that the only value the body has is to enable you to bring your brothers to the bridge with you, and to be released together there.[8]

> Delay will hurt you now more than before, only because you realize it is delay, and that escape from pain is really possible.[9]

> Enter with Him into a holy instant, and there let Him release you.[10]

If this is not real, then no body is real. I am not a body, yet I believe I am somebody. Wayne continued thinking to himself. *This can be interpreted as intended, meaning death is simply a return to Source. But for the fearful it can very easily be interpreted as inciting suicide or killing.*

Death is the moment we leave the suffering experienced in the human realm behind to return to Source. This world is not a friendly or peaceful place for many people. Fear is at every turn for those who perceive it that way, which is the way it has been presented to most of us. Book seven from The Republic *by Plato is a perfect portrayal of this. It need not be this way, though, but it is very difficult to fathom the world any other way.*

There is no explanation why humans are even here on earth. Earth is such a beautiful place if we actually paid attention. Most people perceive the world in a way that can easily be considered the hell Christians speak of. Everyone wants to avoid hell, but what if we are already there because we have created hell on earth? Everyone wants to escape the hell they created in order to attain heaven. But, seeing how beautiful the earth is, how can it be hell? Do humans somehow create a hell from a heavenly earth? Our experience of the world is an entirely different thing than that of the earth.

"Oh, hey!" Wayne interrupted his thoughts to greet his wife, Sue, who walked into the kitchen. "How was your walk?" Wayne asked.

"Good. It's a beautiful day outside. The dogs ran off for a bit, but they eventually came back. They'll probably plop down and rest for a while."

"Can I get you a cup of coffee?"

"Yeah! That would be great."

Wayne stood up from the table and walked over to grab Sue's favorite mug from the coffee mug rack. *World's Greatest Mom!* He read the text on the mug and smiled. Grabbing the coffeepot, he poured hot coffee into the mug and topped it off with a heavy splash of soy milk. He added another splash of soy milk, just in case, and placed the coffee mug in front of Sue. "Here you go. I hope it's hot enough."

Sue grasped the handle with her fingertips and turned the mug toward herself. Hugging the mug with both hands, she held it up to her nose, breathing in the aroma. "Mmm. Smells good. Thanks." Sue smiled and took a sip. "Perfect."

"I have this recurring dream about my mom," Wayne said.

"About what?" Sue replied.

"It's about her passing. Well, it is really about her home and the reminders."

"Oh yeah. That's never an easy thought to process or conversation to have. I think about my parents often. I wish they were here to see the girls." Tears began streaming down her cheeks.

"I'm sorry. I didn't mean to upset you."

"I know you didn't. I just miss them, but it's good to remember them."

"Yeah, your parents were great. We had so many good times with them. I remember when they visited us in Vegas. That was fun!"

"Yeah. It sure was. How about our trip to New York?"

"Oh my gosh! I forgot about that. Do you remember when your dad fell asleep in the lobby of the Hilton hotel?"

Sue shook her head and smiled. "Yeah. That place was busy. There were people everywhere, and it was so loud."

"Yep. And he just sat down in a chair in the hotel lobby and took a nap." Wayne smiled, reliving the memory.

"When we left them at the subway to head home, they were definitely out of their element. I remember the doors closing and the subway car slowly cruising off into the distance. I don't know how they did it, but they made it off the subway and onto the Amtrak train back home."

"Yeah. That was fun. Didn't your mom leave her cell phone on the train, or was that your dad?"

"It was mom. She left it on the subway. Oh well, if that was the worst thing that happened, then it was a huge success. OK. Enough of that. Tell me about your dream."

"Oh yeah. So I walk into her house through the glass sliding door in her sunroom, which I have probably done thousands of times over the forty years since she moved in."

"Yeah, we are blessed to live so close. I am so grateful to be here."

"Yeah, me too. Although I regret that I may not express it often enough. I still tell her once in a while how much I love her and appreciate her unwavering support. She usually says that she knows and that I don't need to tell her. So I stopped expressing my gratitude in words."

"I wouldn't worry about that. She tells me all the time how happy she is seeing the girls and how she enjoys picking them up from school when she can."

"So what remains is a morning greeting and a brief check-in conversation in the afternoon. In the evenings, if she's up to it, we watch TV: *The Andy Griffith Show*, *MASH*, and *Everybody Loves Raymond*. Sometimes we laugh until it hurts. Other times, we just sit in silence together. It's pretty awesome."

"Is that your dream?"

"Uh, no. Sorry." Wayne paused. "This is the dream. The house is empty, and all I have are memories. I miss our nonconversational time together. Being in the presence of one another felt good. Words did not need to be said." Wayne continued, "Then I replay all of the things that happened over the years. I know for a fact that I saved her from making wrong decisions as far as her health was concerned, and she also helped me when I needed it most."

"Yes, you certainly have helped her a great deal. Although I am still not sure how she put up with you when you were younger." Sue smiled, slipping in a snide comment.

"Whatever." Wayne took a sip of his coffee. "Spending so much time around her, I knew what was going on with regard to her health, patterns of sickness, and how to recover. I just don't know if I will ever get past the verbal assault and threats from my brother Alex. That was really fucked up. He said some things that can never be forgiven. Plus, despite their good intentions, my other brothers weren't as clued in to what was happening with her and probably would have endangered her well-being without realizing it."

"Especially since we were in the midst of the pandemic, she could have been seriously harmed," Sue passionately stated.

"Ignorance is the only word that comes to mind. Maybe blind ignorance is better. There are so many people who are ignorant to what really happened. It was a farce," Wayne said. "It's nearly impossible to understand and see the truth through the lies, confusion, and fear. It took me more than ten years to unravel the misinformation about 'germs.'" Wayne raised his hands, gesturing air quotes. "To reveal the truth about health and healing. It goes against everything we were taught in school and raised to believe. The more I learn and reveal the truth, the more it reminds me of the 'Opposite George' episode of *Seinfeld*."

Sue laughed. "Yeah, it is strange how the truth seems to be the opposite of nearly everything we are taught."

"Yep!"

"Of all the times you were there with your mother, to nurse her back to health, especially during the pandemic," Sue paused. "I know she is grateful."

"I realize I kept her safe and did what was best for her. I cared for her and protected her. But I just don't understand how people, still to this day, disregard the lies that are still right in front of them!"

"You're preaching to the choir," she replied. "I understand and feel your frustrations, but you already know that."

"And I readily admit, at the time, I was lost and was still angry from working at Pigeon Financial. It felt like I had PTSD. I am still scarred by how fucked-up that place was, and still is. I don't know if I told you, but I got an email a couple of months ago from someone who was hired and then left after about eight months. He told me how toxic it was, and how he wished he knew the truth about the company and my story before accepting the job. So, yeah, I was in a dark place. But I also know it was probably one of the greatest lessons in my life about human behavior, greed, and abuse."

"I'm sorry that I never understood how bad it was," Sue commented.

"It's OK. There was no way for anyone to fully understand it unless they were there. I am ever grateful that my mom was there to support me when I needed it most. And now her house is empty," Wayne continued.

"In your dream?"

"Yes, sorry. The house is empty in my dream because she is no longer with us. I walk in and I am reminded of all of the ties and memories that were created in that house over so many years. Pictures of my brothers, their kids, my stepfather, his kids, and his grandkids. I look at pictures of my stepdad and tell him how much I love him and wish I had another opportunity to get to know him better. There is a tapestry of past memories woven throughout the house. One person, my mom, kept the tapestry together for so many years. Now that the house is empty, the tapestry falls apart." Wayne paused to reflect. "I'm worried that regret, grievances, hatred, and jealousy will rear their ugly heads, erasing all of the good times."

"Well, let's hope it doesn't come to that."

"Yes, I agree. But the things that were said and done were so fucked-up. Of all the people in the world, Alex was the last one I expected to say the things he did. It is really a sad moment seeing the house empty. After decades and the tapestry of memories that were woven together because of her unwavering love for us and her extended family, it will fall away, and nothing will remain."

Opposite George

> "The world will wash away, and yet this house will stand forever, for its strength lies not within itself alone."[11]
>
> —*A Course in Miracles*

> "This chapter introduces the idea of rebirth or samsara. The Self wears the body as a garment; when the garment is old, it is cast aside and a new one is put on. Thus the soul, or jiva, travels from life to life. Just as death is certain for the living, rebirth is certain for the dead."[12]
>
> — *The Bhagavad Gita*

> "I was a hidden treasure, and I loved to be known, and so I created the worlds both visible and invisible."
>
> —*Islamic mysticism*

The Kindness Lie

"Easter Sunday a few years ago, I had a revelation when I was awakened to a sad truth," Wayne said.

"What do you mean?"

"We teach ourselves and our children a kindness lie."

"OK, what the heck does that mean?"

"I was throwing the softball with Ella and Charlotte. We were joking as we threw the ball around the horn. Eventually, sibling jealously reared its ugly head. I complimented Ella on her catch. Almost instantaneously, Charlotte looked at me and said, 'What about me?'"

"Oh, boy." Sue sighed. "That drives me crazy when they go at each other."

"Yeah, sibling rivalry. My brothers and I used to go at it pretty fiercely," Wayne commented.

"Where was I during all of this?"

"I think you were in the house with everyone else, watching TV, enjoying all of the Easter candy and food, or playing card games. So, on the next throw, Charlotte made a snide remark about Ella's throw. She said something like, 'Nice throw. Maybe next time you can reach me.'"

"Ah, the backhanded compliment." Sue laughed.

"That was the beginning of the end. I looked at Charlotte, and she looked at me. She threw the ball to me, and I said, 'Great throw!' And I meant it, but there was a tinge of sarcasm in my voice. And she noticed it. After that, the sarcastic remarks went around the horn along with the softball. Whenever there was a missed ball or a bad throw, the sarcasm cut through the Easter afternoon air. 'Nice throw' was said in a scathing tone. 'Oh, boy. You actually caught the ball,' soon followed, which was accompanied by a mischievous grin."

"What's wrong with that? That's just basic trash-talking. We all do it."

"I know. But what really bothered me was that, I believe, people find it really difficult to give an honest-to-goodness compliment, especially when it involves siblings," Wayne explained. "So, what I did in that moment, was tell them how I loved them both and that it was time we paid one another a compliment each time the ball was thrown."

"That's a good idea. Did it work?"

"Well ..." Wayne sighed. "Sort of, but not really. It was pretty difficult to simply be nice and give a compliment. Because, when the compliments began to flow, each one was accompanied by a snide comment. Whenever a compliment was paid, it sounded a little corny and felt strange, like a feeling being unsafe or insecure."

"Vulnerable, maybe?"

"Yes, vulnerable. That's it. You know, we always joke with one another and make sarcastic remarks to one another in a lighthearted way. But I never realized how bad it had become. Is it really difficult for someone to pay another person an honest compliment or praise them without a snide remark afterward? I don't think people know how to give an honest-to-goodness compliment or receive one without following it up with a sarcastic remark. People pay compliments in jest, not really meaning it. Or, if they pay a compliment, it is said facetiously, sort of like they are giving up a part of themselves when they say something nice."

"Even worse is when they expect something in return," Sue added.

"Good point. Strings attached," Wayne replied.

"Yep."

"So, when someone dropped the ball or made a bad throw, a compliment was blurted. 'Good try! You'll get the next one!' Which felt great. But eventually, it just became silly. We would blurt out things like, 'Great job!' 'Nice try! You'll get the next one!' or 'Keep it up. You're doing great!' and 'You gave it your best!'"

"So, that's great, right?"

"Yeah, it was. But we couldn't help but laugh at how silly it sounded."

"Well, you were just having fun. People joke and pick on one another all the time."

"Yeah, I guess. Parents and coaches say they want kids to get better and support them along the way, but when a kid fails or makes a mistake, our culture tends to reprimand them rather than support them. We believe in demeaning someone when they make a mistake, as though that is a motivating factor so they will improve. It's an oxymoron!"

Wayne continued, "Think about when someone receives a compliment. They are usually expecting a snide remark or criticism to follow the compliment. And we have grown to accept it. It's shit like, 'You did great, but ...' 'Your work is excellent, but ...' How can someone's work be great and also not great? How can someone do excellent work that's not excellent? It was either great, or it wasn't."

"I don't think we have a choice. It's not possible to just praise someone. There has to be room for improvement," Sue added.

"I agree, but not the way we approach improvement," Wayne replied. "We do this in all parts of life: school, sports, careers, and relationships. They say to build them up so you can tear them down. People don't like criticism by itself, so we soften them up with some bullshit compliment so we can then tear them apart with criticism. And people are unable to accept a compliment because they expect criticism will immediately follow it."

"Well, I think that's all perspective, which you taught me. The criticism is not as bad as you make it out to be. If I didn't receive feedback from other people, I would not know what I needed to focus on and improve on. I think it is very powerful and beneficial."

"Sure. It's about perspective. Maybe because of my past experiences, I approach it—or receive it—differently than other people."

"Yep. You certainly do," Sue remarked. "One approach can work really well for one person, but for another, it might make things worse."

"Yes. I think my point is that we find it easier to follow our egoic tendencies by grasping onto and being drawn to fearful things: failure, death, and devastation. And when we cast these egoic tendencies onto others, this is when it becomes somewhat tragic."

Wayne grabbed another cup of coffee and refilled Sue's cup. He sat back down, and they talked a while longer.

Opposite George

> "It is because we don't know who we are, because we are unaware that the Kingdom of Heaven is within us, that we behave in the generally silly, the often insane, the sometimes criminal ways that are so characteristically human."[13]
>
> — *The Perennial Philosophy*

> "Miracles are teaching devices for demonstrating it is as blessed to give as to receive. They simultaneously increase the strength of the giver and supply strength to the receiver."[14]
>
> —*A Course in Miracles*

Do as You Are Told

"So do as you are told."

"What?" Sue replied, caught off guard by Wayne's comment which came out of left field.

"You are born, go to school, get a job, make a living, and your life will be perfect! Do as you are told. The moment you do not do as you are told, everything begins to unravel. No longer making any sense, you begin to question everything. Do you get back in line and do as you are told, or do you keep searching to find an entirely different existence, living an entirely different life?"

"Uh, I don't know."

"Here, read book seven from Plato's *The Republic*." Wayne slid his computer across the kitchen table, turning the screen toward Sue. "Start reading this. I'm going to the bathroom. I'll be back in a bit, and hopefully you will have read most of it."

Sue began to read as Wayne stood up from the table to go to the bathroom.

> "And now, I said, let me show in a figure how far our nature is enlightened or unenlightened: —Behold! Human beings living in a underground den, which has a mouth open towards the light and reaching all along the den; here they have been from their childhood, and have their legs and necks chained so that they cannot move, and can only see before them, being prevented by the chains from turning 'round their heads. Above and behind them a fire is blazing at a distance, and between the fire and the prisoners there is a raised way; and you will see, if you look, a low wall built along the way, like

the screen which marionette players have in front of them, over which they show the puppets.

I see.

And do you see, I said, men passing along the wall carrying all sorts of vessels, and statues and figures of animals made of wood and stone and various materials, which appear over the wall? Some of them are talking, others silent.

You have shown me a strange image, and they are strange prisoners.

Like ourselves, I replied; and they see only their own shadows, or the shadows of one another, which the fire throws on the opposite wall of the cave?

True, he said; how could they see anything but the shadows if they were never allowed to move their heads?

And of the objects which are being carried in like manner they would only see the shadows?

Yes, he said.

And if they were able to converse with one another, would they not suppose that they were naming what was actually before them?

Very true.

And suppose further that the prison had an echo which came from the other side, would they not be sure to fancy when one of the passersby spoke that the voice which they heard came from the passing shadow?

No question, he replied.

To them, I said, the truth would be literally nothing but the shadows of the images.

That is certain.

And now look again, and see what will naturally follow it, the prisoners are released and disabused of their error. At first, when any of them is liberated and compelled suddenly to stand up and turn his neck 'round and walk and look towards the light, he will suffer sharp pains; the glare will distress him, and he will be unable to see the realities of which in his former state he had seen the shadows; and then conceive someone saying to him, that what he saw before was an illusion, but that now, when he is approaching nearer to being and his eye is turned towards more real existence, he has a clearer vision, what will be his reply? And you may further imagine that his instructor is pointing to the objects as they pass and requiring him to name them, will he not be perplexed? Will he not fancy that the shadows which he formerly saw are truer than the objects which are now shown to him?

Far truer.

And if he is compelled to look straight at the light, will he not have a pain in his eyes which will make him turn away to take and take in the objects of vision which he can see, and which he will conceive to be in reality clearer than the things which are now being shown to him?

True, he said.

And suppose once more, that he is reluctantly dragged up a steep and rugged ascent, and held fast until he's forced into the presence of the sun himself, is he not likely to be pained and irritated? When he approaches the light his eyes will be dazzled, and he will not be able to see anything at all of what are now called realities.

Not all in a moment, he said.

He will require to grow accustomed to the sight of the upper world. And first he will see the shadows best, next the reflections of men and other objects in the water, and then the objects themselves; then he will gaze upon the light of the moon and the stars and the spangled heaven; and he will see the sky and the stars by night better than the sun or the light of the sun by day?

Certainly.

Last of he will be able to see the sun, and not mere reflections of him in the water, but he will see him in his own proper place, and not in another; and he will contemplate him as he is.

Certainly.

He will then proceed to argue that this is he who gives the season and the years, and is the guardian of all that is in the visible world, and in a certain way the cause of all things which he and his fellows have been accustomed to behold?

Clearly, he said, he would first see the sun and then reason about him.

And when he remembered his old habitation, and the wisdom of the den and his fellow prisoners, do you not suppose that he would felicitate himself on the change, and pity them?

Certainly, he would.

And if they were in the habit of conferring honours among themselves on those who were quickest to observe the passing shadows and to remark which of them went before, and which followed after, and which were together; and who were therefore best able to draw conclusions as to the future, do you think that he would care for such honours and glories, or envy the possessors of them? Would he not say with Homer,

Better to be the poor servant of a poor master, and to endure anything, rather than think as they do and live after their manner?

Yes, he said, I think that he would rather suffer anything than entertain these false notions and live in this miserable manner.

Imagine once more, I said, such an one coming suddenly out of the sun to be replaced in his old situation; would he not be certain to have his eyes full of darkness?

To be sure, he said.

And if there were a contest, and he had to compete in measuring the shadows with the prisoners who had never moved out of the den, while his sight was still weak, and before his eyes had become steady (and the time which would be needed to acquire this new habit of sight might be very considerable) would he not be ridiculous? Men would say of him that up he went and down he came without his eyes; and that it was better not even to think of ascending; and if any one tried to loose another and lead him up to the light, let them only catch the offender, and they would put him to death.

No question, he said.

> This entire allegory, I said, you may now append, dear Glaucon, to the previous argument; the prison-house is the world of sight, the light of the fire is the sun, and you will not misapprehend me if you interpret the journey upwards to be the ascent of the soul into the intellectual world according to my poor belief, which, at your desire, I have expressed whether rightly or wrongly God knows. But, whether true or false, my opinion is that in the world of knowledge the idea of good appears last of all, and is seen only with an effort; and, when seen, is also inferred to be the universal author of all things beautiful and right, parent of light and of the lord of light in this visible world, and the immediate source of reason and truth in the intellectual; and that this is the power upon which he who would act rationally, either in public or private life must have his eye fixed.
>
> I agree, he said, as far as I am able to understand you.
>
> Moreover, I said, you must not wonder that those who attain to this beatific vision are unwilling to descend to human affairs; for their souls are ever hastening into the upper world where they desire to dwell; which desire of theirs is very natural, if our allegory may be trusted."[15]

A few minutes later, Wayne walked back into the kitchen and topped off his coffee. "Can I get you another coffee?" He asked.

"Nah. Actually, can you warm up my cup for me?"

"Sure thing." Wayne smiled and grabbed her coffee mug. He popped open the microwave oven door and pressed the *BEVERAGE* button. Sue continued to read book seven of *The Republic*. A little over a minute later, the oven beeped. He pressed the button to open the door to the microwave oven and grabbed Sue's coffee mug.

"Here you go," Wayne said as he placed the mug in front of Sue.

Opposite George

> "As I see it, you are all on a stage performing. There is no reality about your comings and goings. And your problems are so unreal." [16]
>
> — *I Am That*

Who Are You?

"So what'd you think? Have you read that before?" Wayne asked.

"Wow! Uh, no, I haven't, but I've heard about it," Sue replied.

"Fascinating. Isn't it?"

"Uh, yeah. And sadly, it makes sense."

"Yeah, the pandemic confirmed for me how people have no clue about reality, or their lives being programmed by mass media and the puppet show that has been played out in front of them."

"Which creates what they believe to be true," Sue interrupted.

"Yes, creating their reality, or life experience."

"Yes!" she exclaimed.

"I should go back and read book seven again. It's always good to go back and reread things, because I catch stuff I missed the first time around. I'm going to change direction slightly." Wayne paused and quickly resumed with a question. "Do you realize you own nothing?" he asked.

"What are you talking about?" Sue asked.

Wayne's phone started ringing. He grabbed his iPhone and looked at the screen. "It's Gary. Hold on." Wayne pressed his right-hand thumb on the green phone icon at the bottom of his screen and slid it to the right. "Gary! What's up, my friend?"

"Wayne Renroc, the author. How are you?" Gary asked.

"I'm great. Hey, I'm sitting here talking with Sue. I have you on speakerphone."

"Hey, Sue! How are you?"

"Things are good. I hope the same with you," Sue replied.

"Yes, everyone's happy and healthy," Gary said. "I didn't mean to interrupt, but I'm in your neck of the woods and wanted to see if you'd like to grab a coffee."

"Yeah! That would be great. Let's meet at Burlap and Bean. What time?"

"How about in about fifteen minutes?"

"Sounds great."

"Before you hang up, you called at the perfect time. We were just in the middle of a deep conversation, and we'd like your opinion."

"Uh-oh," Gary mumbled. "What's up?"

"Do you realize you own nothing?" Wayne asked the same question he'd just posed to Sue.

"What?" Gary replied.

"You own nothing. I own nothing. And we gave away all of our freedom, identities, and things we value."

"Wow! Do you really want to ask me that?"

"Yep, I do." Wayne smiled.

"Don't worry, Gary," Sue said with a slight laugh. "He just asked me the same question, and I responded the same way you did."

"Oh, OK." Gary sighed.

"Before I head out to meet you, do you have a minute?" Wayne asked Gary.

"I do. Lay it on me," Gary responded.

"Great. So we really don't own anything, and the things we own really own us. We are slaves to the things we have. We define ourselves and base our identities on our things and accomplishments."

"Well, that makes sense," Gary interjected.

"OK. And what happens when your Google, iCloud, or other accounts are canceled or deleted? Or, what if your things break or are stolen?"

"I never really thought about it. I guess I'd back it up from the cloud," Gary said.

"There is no more cloud." Wayne paused. "What then? They keep it all. Your info, photos, habits, rituals, personal life ... everything!"

Sue rolled her eyes and took a sip of her coffee.

"OK. That's not going to happen," Gary responded.

"That's what I say, Gary. That won't happen." Sue leaned over to speak into the phone.

"You're probably right, but just go along with me," Wayne continued. "When the lights go out, and you no longer have access to anything, what will you do? Who are you? I'm saying your photos are wiped out. Your passwords are gone, and you cannot log in to any of your accounts. No access to your banking, your online brokerage account, everything."

"Well, that would really suck. I guess I would be screwed." Gary paused. "But, like I said, that's not going to happen."

"Fair enough. Let me put it this way: who are you without your device? Have you ever left home without your smartphone? It's a strange feeling, isn't it?"

Sue chuckled. "I've done that, and I'm not going to lie. It's awkward. I need my phone to know where I'm going. Plus, I have no way of contacting people."

"You can't order coffee on the way to work," Wayne interjected. "Actually, you can't order coffee, because if you walk into the store these days, the employees have no clue how to talk to people or how to take an order from an actual person."

"Yeah, I walked into a coffee shop a while back and wanted to place an order at the counter. The kid working there told me I had to order it on the app, and they wouldn't take my order. I was in the damn coffee shop, and I couldn't order coffee!" Gary exclaimed.

"Plus, some of these places don't accept cash," Sue added.

"I've become so reliant on my iPhone that I really don't know how to get anywhere without it," Wayne added. "It's really disturbing to see our kids rely on their phones for everything. They're never without their iPhones."

"Yeah, but remember when home computer video games came out, and they said they were the next thing that would ruin us? It didn't," Gary commented.

"Are you sure about that?" Wayne asked. "Who are we without technology? What about the news? Would you feel a little out of touch if you didn't read or watch the news? Maybe a little disconnected?"

"Yeah," Gary answered.

Sue shook her head at Gary's response because she knew where Wayne was headed.

"It scares the crap out of people to not be in the know," Wayne continued. "We have become so mindless. We're afraid of missing out and have become addicted to the news, the latest social media post, or the latest Netflix series. We believe we must be connected at all times, and we need to be the first with breaking news and the latest gossip."

"But I don't pay attention to that garbage. The latest gossip, I mean," Gary stated. "Although I do watch the news every morning. I listen for the weather report and the morning traffic."

Wayne stepped in. "I don't. In fact, I haven't for years, and nothing has changed. I haven't missed anything. Actually, I feel much better about the world because I'm no longer watching the mindless, fearmongering newscasts."

"Well, I guess it's all about what we choose to focus on. I don't pay attention to the bullshit, like the daily shootings, deaths, and tragedies," Gary added.

"Well, you must be aware of it or pay attention if you know they still report on it. You may not realize how addictive it is, but the ego feeds off of this mindless and meaningless emotion. We are so addicted that we cannot fathom existence without the allure of these egoic tendencies. Our reality has been molded and created from the fear, hatred, war, killing, and separateness streamed before our eyes on the screens in front of our faces twenty-four seven."

"I agree with that. The twenty-four seven news is ridiculous. But I have to watch something."

"Hey, Gary," Sue interrupted. "Have you ever just turned it off and walked away?"

"Nah. That's not going to happen. I need to know what's going on."

"No, you don't," Wayne interjected. "You only believe you need to know what's going on."

"Don't worry, you are not going to miss anything," Sue added.

"And even if you did, someone always reminds you. Take my word for it. Someone will always let you know what's going on," Wayne said.

"So you really don't watch TV or the news?" Gary asked.

"Yep. No news," Wayne said.

"We got rid of cable a while ago," Sue added. "We do watch movies and sports, though."

"Yeah, but I'm tired of the same boring plots and storylines," Wayne added. "It's the same story over and over again; just different characters, different settings, with the same idiotic and mindless storyline."

Wayne continued, "It isn't easy to turn it off and walk away at first. But, boy, it is worth it when you do! The emotions experienced are similar to how someone feels when they stop drinking. For the longest time, you fall for the lie that you cannot have fun unless you drink or cannot relax unless you drink. When in social situations, you feel the urge to have a drink. In fact, you become anxious and uncomfortable if you don't have a drink in your hand. But eventually, the awkwardness fades. This is the moment you realize that you had fallen for a lie. Drinking is used as a crutch and is an ingenious way to keep people from truly awakening to their true potential. In fact, the pressure is so strong that people live their entire lives not knowing there is another way to exist and experience life. Your realization will be that nearly everything you believed was wrong. Most everything in life is quite the opposite of what you have been led to believe. Even falling for the ludicrous lie that you can only be happy or have fun when drinking. If you are stressed out, you then fall for the lie that drinking will solve all of your problems. Drinking never made anyone's stress go away. Maybe it numbed the feeling of stress for a moment, but when you come to, your stress is still faithfully by your side." Wayne continued, "And, unfortunately, I know what I am talking about."

"Yep. You really had fun in college. Maybe a little too much fun."

"Sorry to end the fun, but I am heading out to pick up Abby," Sue said. "Gary, it was great to catch up. Say hi to Bella and the kids."

"I will. Great talking with you," Gary said.

"I'll be back in a bit," Sue said to Wayne, giving him a kiss on the lips.

"I'm going to head out and meet Gary, so I'll see you later," Wayne said to Sue.

"OK, have fun. See ya next time, Gary!"

"OK," Gary replied.

"So what were we talking about?" Wayne asked Gary.

"College," Sue said as she walked out the door.

"Oh yeah. I had too much fun," Wayne said to Gary. "But it wasn't all rainbows and unicorns. I drank, hoping to wash away my anger and stress. It never worked, though. I just felt worse in the morning, with a hangover to exacerbate things."

"But you sure had your fun. That's what I like about you. You don't seem to care, and you do whatever you want, regardless of the consequences. I could never do that."

"Well, everyone believes the bullshit on television, in Hollywood, and on social media. And it becomes our reality. The majority of people in the world believe they need the news. They wake up every day to watch the news. To find out what's going on in the world: the weather, the traffic, crime, and on and on. I stopped watching the news and reading the paper nearly twenty years ago. And I have not missed a thing! I have not listened to the traffic report or the weather forecast for years. And the world is a much more beautiful place because of it! One of the biggest lies in the world's history reared its ugly head in 2020. And practically everyone on the planet believed it, despite it being fabricated. Yet it worked. It became reality for the entire planet! It was impossible for it not to enter your realm of consciousness." Wayne grabbed his keys and took a quick pit stop at the bathroom before leaving.

"I still don't understand how you can say it was a lie," Gary said.

"I know you don't. That's the power of training the mind. There's usually a glimmer of truth hidden in all the lies, but most everyone has no clue that most of it is bullshit, and they go about their lives."

"Dude, are you taking a leak?"

Wayne flushed the toilet and continued talking. "Yeah, sorry. I had to go to the bathroom before I left."

"Next time, hang up or hit the mute button."

"Got it," Wayne replied. "Once you see it, you can no longer ignore it. It's like one of those pictures in which you see one thing, but there is an entirely different image on the page."

"I remember the old lady painting, and when you look closer at the image, there's also a picture of a young woman." Gary added.

"Yep, that's the one. The moment you see it, you cannot go back and unsee it. So, the moment you look past the lies and see the truth, you no longer see the lies but only the truth. The lies are still there, but you no longer see them. Every now and then, you are reminded they are there. When this happens, it momentarily sucks you back into the pits of hell, reminding you of what the rest of the world perceives as their reality. Do you remember what Nazi propaganda minister Joseph Goebbels said?"

"Yeah," Gary sighed. "I do. He said, 'If you repeat a lie often enough, it becomes the truth.'"

"Precisely, and that sums up the pandemic. This world that we live in and experience would not be so full of anger, violence, and hatred if we simply turned off the noise and our devices. Ideally, things would improve if humans stopped chasing fear, death, and hatred on the news, in the headlines, on social media, and in Hollywood." Wayne put his jacket on and walked out the door. He hopped into his car and started the engine.

"It's another brilliant plan for the sadistic. To keep our faces in our devices so we never wake up to our true potential and power. There is hope, though. If everyone began reporting on and talking about a world we all dream of and desire, one without hatred, greed or fear, our entire existence would change. But sadly, we are too far gone for that to happen, and the next best solution would be a mass extinction event."

"Dude. You're crazy! Please don't tell me you believe that. How in the world could you say that?"

"What do you mean?"

"That's awful!"

"Is it? Or are you saying that because you are afraid of death? Look at the world. It's a fucking shit show. People are so stupid and ignorant. The only way of saving humanity would be a mass extinction event. Even if this idiot, Elon Musk, were to colonize Mars, all that would be accomplished would be a relocation of the fearful and ignorant people to another planet to spread our fear and stupidity. We're like a cancer. Colonizing another planet is ludicrous!" Wayne shifted his car into drive and pulled out of the driveway.

"My life has not changed since I stopped watching the news, other than becoming much better."

"Are you sure about that, Wayne? Are you really better?"

"Well, yes and no. I am still figuring a lot of shit out. But from the standpoint of the news, or no news, I get to where I need to go without watching the traffic report. My day doesn't change because I haven't watched the weather report. If it's chilly outside, I put on a coat or wear a sweater. I don't need a dramatic weather report to figure that out. I haven't missed a thing! In fact, the only things that are missing from my life are the anxiety and fear which go hand in hand with the news."

"But how do you get by, day to day? Don't you need to know what's going on to do your job?"

"Fuck!" Wayne yelled. "Sorry, my Bluetooth was connecting in my car, and I missed what you were saying. Sorry."

"I was asking how do you get by day to day? Don't you need to know what's going on to do your job?"

"Not really. Plus, if there is something urgent, I will be notified somehow and someway. What's pathetic and quite laughable is working in financial services and seeing the same bullshit over and over again. Nothing has changed in the twenty-five years I have been in this field."

"So you mean to tell me you don't watch the news? Like CNBC? Or listen to Bloomberg?" Gary kept on prying.

Wayne laughed. "Why would I? Although Sue reminds me that there is always a hint of truth hidden somewhere in the lies and bullshit portrayed on the news, television, and social media. Let me be clear, though: I do listen to webinars and podcasts, and I read articles to stay abreast of the trends in my industry, which have been the same repeatable trends year after year. I find it comical to see the same patterns repeated over and over again. We're like puppets doing the same thing, chasing the latest drama and fear. It amazes me that people don't pick up on the cues, which are more obvious and obnoxious every year. I mean, how can anyone miss it? Humans spread fear like a disease. We are more than happy to share the latest drama, horror story, or devastation with others. We feed off of fear like fucking addicts. We don't know what to do without it! People drink or get high to disconnect from the world. Then they wake up the next day, hungover or strung out, needing to get a drink or another high to disconnect again. Pay attention. Now that I have disconnected from the world, I am more connected than ever before. The difference is, when I wake up the next day, I am not hungover or strung out, and I don't need to get drunk or high again to disconnect. I am permanently disconnected from the toxicity and bullshit. Because of that, I am more connected than ever, and it is wonderful. This world is a beautiful place! The next time you walk outside, look up. Look up at the beautiful blue sky above, and enjoy watching the clouds floating by, look at the sunrise or sunset. You will see miracles all around you."

"Didn't you once say the sun never sets nor rises?"

"I did, and it's absolutely true. It never sets nor rises; we just perceive it as though it sets and rises. As the earth rotates, the sun comes into view—a sunrise—and then goes out of view—a sunset. A tree grows without a device and without technology. A flower blooms every spring without the need of a device. It remains truly connected to nature and Source. All of it happens without a device. That is being connected! I walk out my front door every morning and need to remind myself to look up and around me. The entire world could be ablaze, and I wouldn't even notice because I didn't take the time to look up and observe the beauty surrounding me."

Opposite George

> When I let go of what I am, I become what I might be.
>
> —Lao Tzu

> "Everybody sees the world through the idea he has of himself."[17]
>
> — *I Am That*

> "It teaches that we can become free by giving up not material things, but selfish attachments to material things—and, more important, to people. It asks us to renounce not the enjoyment of life, but the clinging to selfish enjoyment whatever it may cost others."[18]
>
> — *The Bhagavad Gita*

"You have the right to work, but never to the fruit of work. You should never engage in action for the sake of reward, nor should you long for inaction. Perform work in this world, Arjuna, as a man established within himself—without selfish attachments, and alike in success and defeat. For yoga is perfect evenness of mind."[19]

— *The Bhagavad Gita*

"The wise endowed with equanimity of intellect, abandon attachment to the fruits of actions, which bind one to the cycle of life and death. By working in such consciousness, they attain the state beyond all suffering."[20]

— *The Bhagavad Gita*

"Those who are motivated only by desire for the fruits of action are miserable, for they are constantly anxious about the results of what they do. When consciousness is unified, however, all vain anxiety is left behind. There is no cause for worry, whether things go well or ill."[21]

— *The Bhagavad Gita*

Don't Change the World. Instead, Change Yourself.

Wayne arrived at the coffee shop and parked on the side street. "Dude, I'm at the coffee shop," Wayne said as he got out of his car. He closed the car door, pressed the button on his key fob to lock the vehicle, and hurriedly walked to meet Gary. "Walking in now. I'm hanging up."

He walked through the front door and spied Gary sitting at a table in the side room. "Hey, Gary!" Wayne said enthusiastically as he approached Gary.

Gary stood up from the table. They shook hands, and Wayne gave Gary a big hug. "It's so great to see you. This is a special treat to catch up in person!"

"Yeah. I wasn't sure what you had going on today, but I figured I'd call, and here we are. You look great!"

"Thanks, man. So do you! How are Bella and the kids?"

"They're great. I think I gave you an update the last time we spoke, but they're doing well."

"Awesome," Wayne replied.

"Can I get you a coffee?" Gary asked.

"Yeah, that would be great. I see you already ordered, so I'll get the next one."

"Sounds good."

Gary walked over to the counter and ordered a cup of coffee for Wayne. He walked back over to the table while they waited for Wayne's coffee.

"So what deep discussion were you and Sue in when I called?" Gary asked.

"Well, you got a taste of what it was about."

"I did." Gary smiled, shaking his head. "You always go deep and ask questions that others don't."

"Rattling cages, as you always say." Wayne smiled.

"Yep, rattling cages. What are you rattling now?"

"Change."

"Change?"

"Yeah, change."

"What about change?" Gary asked.

"Well, it's more about changing the world. We need to stop trying to change the world and wanting to change people. These efforts will prove fruitless and quite frustrating. So, instead, we can change ourselves. What we need to focus on is the change within. In that moment, our perspective of the world and of others will change."

"Sort of like the 'Serenity Prayer.' 'God, grant me the serenity to accept the things I cannot change, courage to change the things I can, and wisdom to know the difference,'" Gary said.

"Yes! And we are able to change things for the better through mini dharma/Karma."

"Huh?"

"Mini dharma/Karma. At death and rebirth, we can pick up from our prior lifetime and experience the thoughts we held deeply. Each day is like a lifetime. We experience the day through our senses and go to bed with takeaways from the day. When we wake up, it is a new beginning and another chance to improve. This is a mini dharma/Karma. But most people live their lives more like a mini crucifixion/resurrection instead. We experience life in a storyline very similar to Jesus Christ's crucifixion and resurrection. Jesus was hated and despised for his beliefs, which were not in line with the church and state. Not much has changed in today's world. People will still hate and judge those who do not comply with the church and state. I'm not talking about criminal activities. I am talking about those who step out of line in order to better humanity. I'm talking about stepping out of line for good, for God. When someone does not do as they are told, or when their behavior is not in line with the rest of the herd, they are quickly judged, outcast, and often crucified."

"Gary, order's up! Order for Gary is ready!" The barista roared from behind the counter.

"Hold on. That's me," Wayne walked over to pick up his coffee. He sat back down at the table and continued. "One more thing I find quite comical. A friend of my daughter Madeline asked Sue to be her sponsor, or godparent, for her induction onto the Catholic faith during the Easter Sunday vigil."

"That's great, but you aren't Catholic."

"Yep. Sue was happy to do so, but the church wouldn't allow her to be a sponsor because she is not of the Catholic faith. Sue is a technically a Christian, and the last time I checked, we all prayed to the same Christ. But, because their version of the Bible and story of Jesus Christ is different, despite praying to and honoring the same Son of God, a letter of permission was required. Come on! This is not how God works. God is all-loving and all-powerful, yet He divides us because the way I pray to Him and honor Him is different from the way you do it? They do say God works in mysterious ways. Maybe this is one of those mysterious but fucked-up ways."

"Well, uh …" Gary did not know what to say.

"This certainly was not what Jesus was doing and saying. He realized there were mockers, there were those who were confused, and then, more importantly, there were the believers. He didn't curse the mockers or those who were confused by damning them to hell because they didn't follow him or believe in him. No, he just went on preaching to help awaken people to the truth. And if they decided they wanted to become believers and followers, he didn't ask for a permission slip. He welcomed them with open arms."

"Good point. I believe you are being a little harsh, though. Don't lose sight of all of the good. I do so much with the church, and it has served me well."

"Thank you for the reminder, Gary. I do believe it has served you well, and many others. I believe in it too, but I do not need to be converted or to devote myself to one faith to awaken to higher awareness, even God consciousness."

"OK. Fair enough. I can live with that."

"Well, as I say this, I acknowledge that my resistance is from fear, which is an egoic tendency. The ego does not want us to awaken to higher consciousness, because that means there will not be a need for the ego. So any resistance I feel is the ego fighting for its existence. The moment I awaken to higher awareness, the ego will die. With that understanding ..." Wayne paused. "What if the story of Jesus is just that, a story making fools of us all as we wait for his second coming?"

"Whoa! Hold on, Wayne," Gary responded. "You're taking it a little too far!"

"Am I really, Gary? You've said that those who dedicate their lives to him are doing so in a sort of blind faith that he will return. And if he doesn't, we're all fools."

"I did say that," Gary acknowledged.

"You know that I only ask these questions to seek answers and better understand life. Of course, there has yet to be an answer, just speculation, belief and a lot of hope. I do believe that Jesus could heal and perform miracles. I also know and believe that we can do the same as Jesus did. He was trying to teach us that we all have the Kingdom of God within ourselves. So, yes, you are all fools if you are waiting for one person in the entire world to return and save you. Sort of like Santa Claus delivering presents all over the world in one night."

"What? He can't not return."

"Why?"

"Because it says he will return."

"What if he doesn't? Plus, your faith says that I won't be saved because I don't believe in your version of the story. But, despite my belief in Jesus Christ, your faith will leave me at the gates of hell because I didn't choose your story versus the thousands of other stories about Jesus? And what about the rest of the world? Those who believe in the Buddha or Lord Krishna? Are they all really doomed to hell unless they convert?"

"Well, I don't know about the other religions. But, yes, you have to repent, renounce your sins, and believe in order to be saved."

"Well, that's another reason I won't dedicate myself to one faith, because that's just narrow-minded, fear-based, and silly. Although, if someone finds a faith that serves them well, that's wonderful. But it goes off the rails the moment they try to convert people or say their faith is the best and the only way. I wouldn't doom you to hell because you don't believe in what I believe in. And Jesus didn't do this, either! It's pretty clear he was saying he will return the moment you wake up to the Kingdom of God within yourself. This power is within each of us. This is the second coming of Christ. Stop looking up to the clouds for Jesus or God to descend from the heavens and save you. He is not going to show up at your front door and save you. It is up to each and every one of us to awaken to and align with higher awareness or Christ consciousness. We can do it, even with the numerous of versions of God, Christ, the Buddha, Prince Arjuna, Lord Krishna, and so on. As long as we see the common thread shared between all of them. So, instead of saying my faith is better than yours—which is not how God sees it—we open our eyes and recognize the similarities at the core of each belief."

"OK, I can get on board with that."

"Divide and conquer."

"What? Why did you say that?"

"Because it is easy to conquer and control the human race when they remain divided. The church does this as well with all their different religions and versions of the Bible. If we remain divided, fearful, and ignorant, we will never enter the Kingdom of God. It's a brilliant plan of the sadistic. For anyone who truly believes in God and knows God, they know God would not demand a permission slip to love Him and honor Him or the Son of God. This is just another ludicrous human behavior or egoic tendency. Plus, if anyone were truly aligned with higher consciousness, they would not have experienced the pandemic. Those who are true healers and believers would not have put up plexiglass walls and worn diapers on their faces while worshiping in the house of God. Jesus did not behave this way. Sin does not enter the house of God, but it clearly did in 2020, and it still does. If they were truly connected with Him, they would not have seen any of it. Higher consciousness is a level of enlightenment in which the world fades away and there are no such things as pandemics, disease, or death. When you step back and look at the common threads at the core of the Buddha's and Jesus Christ's beliefs and teachings, this is precisely what they taught." Wayne paused to take a drink of water. "OK. This bears repeating, Gary. Jesus Christ was crucified for his beliefs, which were not the beliefs of the church nor of the state. The crowds could not think for themselves, and they followed the herd. Because of their ignorance and fear, they killed the Son of God."

"You know, Wayne, your words are harsh and hard to hear. But …"

"I figured you would say that," Wayne interrupted.

"Hold on, Wayne, I wasn't finished. As I was saying, the more I reflect on His life, and the more you share about the life of the Buddha and the story of the Bhagavad Gita, the more it opens my eyes."

Wayne was caught off guard by Gary's comments. "Wow! That's great to hear. Thanks, Gary."

"Believe it or not, I listen to what you have to say. You are a really smart dude, smarter than most people, and the things you know and understand are beyond me."

"Thanks, Gary. When you look at it, the storyline that practically every Hollywood movie spits out and Netflix generates follows a very similar theme. There's the beginning. Jesus's birth and early life. All is well. His years as a young adult are a mystery, maybe he's out discovering the world. No one knows. When he is older, conflict arises; Jesus performs miracles, which goes against the wishes of the church and the state. There is talk of the Messiah performing miracles and teaching his gospel which is unwelcome. Hatred and anger ensue from the church, the Roman Empire, and the people."

"Not all people," Gary interjected.

"Yes. Not all people," Wayne said in agreement. "Jesus is arrested, imprisoned, brutally beaten, and tortured. His loved ones and disciples try to save him. They weep as they witness the brutality. Eventually, Jesus is left to die on the cross. Upon Jesus's death, the earth shakes, and this is the beginning of revenge. Then Jesus is resurrected. His body vanishes from his grave. Everyone is amazed and perplexed that he has risen. Now all await the Messiah's return. And when he does return, humanity will be saved. That pretty much sums up the typical plot and storyline for nearly every movie and television show spit out by the Hollywood machine. Beginning, happiness, tragedy, suffering, hate, revenge, and happy ending."

Opposite George

> "The world will end in joy, because it is a place of sorrow. When joy has come, the purpose of the world has gone. The world will end in peace, because it is a place of war. When peace has come, what is the purpose of the world? The world will end in laughter, because it is a place of tears. Where there is laughter, who can longer weep?"[22]
>
> — *A Course in Miracles*

Near-Life Experience

"Dude, have you ever read stories about people having near-death experiences?"

"Yeah. Why?"

"Well, have you ever heard of an NLE?"

"A what?"

"A near-life experience?"

"Nope. What the heck is a near-life experience?"

"I'm glad you asked," Wayne smirked.

"Oh, boy. What are you going to tell me about now?"

"Most people are so afraid of dying that they spend their entire lives fearing and avoiding, or preventing, death, and therefore, they never truly live. That is what is called a near-life experience."

"That's funny! A little sad, but funny."

"People are filled with so much fear and anxiety, it causes them to miss their lives. They never truly live. Even those who are seemingly successful. They are always looking over their shoulders, fearing the worst, and they should all over themselves."

"What?"

"They 'should' all over themselves. Like shit all over themselves but 'should' all over themselves. Get it?"

"Yeah, I've heard that before. They spend their lives saying they should have done this, or they should have done that."

Wayne added, "But they didn't, because it was too dangerous, it cost too much money, they were afraid they might get hurt or sick, and on and on. People spend their lives avoiding death and making sure they are safe, causing them to miss life. That's an NLE, near-life experience.

"We spend so much of our lives chasing things so we can live and enjoy life. But then we worry about it not being enough, not having enough, or that someone else has something better, and we chase after the latest and greatest thing. We end up protecting the things we accumulate because we believe in scarcity and are afraid someone will take them away.

"The awesome things we own end up owning us. Like the prison warden who ends up becoming the prisoner. Plus, we are being sold a bogus bag of goods when we always say that we have responsibilities, and we must work and sacrifice in order to have a good life. That's bullshit!

"We can have a perfectly fine life without sacrificing, having to accumulate, or hoard, which creates the need to protect everything at all costs. Even worse, people like to brag and boast about their wonderful things and amazing accomplishments. While at the same time, we dread our jobs, despise the people we work with, hate our marriages, even our kids, because we want a better life, or it isn't enough. That's all fuel for the ego which is supported by the media. When you truly look at it, life is pretty amazing as it is! How could it get any better? But apparently, it is so bad that we have to accumulate all of these things to make it better, get the latest car, the latest iPhone, blah, blah, blah."

Wayne took a sip of his coffee and continued, "Is there ever a point at which we say, 'All done! I'm finished!' and enjoy all of the things we've accumulated? It seems we have to keep working in order to protect the things we accumulate, or we have to accumulate more, chasing the next high and the next ego-boosting toy. We're just feeding the ego. Then we show off the things we have to everyone else, looking for their approval to validate our empty existence and who we are. And, God forbid, someone has something cooler than we do! We will feel the bite of envy and want the same thing for ourselves. Do we ever really mature after elementary school age? Then what about the TWD, the walking dead, who are like mindlessness man? They are so lost, with their faces glued to their devices, following everyone else and doing what they are told.

"People sacrifice their lives in the name of fear and the ego, truly missing life. Being able to fully enjoy life eludes most of us because we are always looking over our shoulders or around the corner, fearing death, scarcity, or devastation. Man will do anything to cheat death, even miss their own life."

"But didn't you say that was the Buddha's enlightenment? He realized and accepted suffering as a natural part of life. Because it sounds like that is what you just described to me," Gary asked.

"Ah, yes. Good catch." Wayne smiled. "It really is about attachment, which the Buddha taught. Or maybe I should say unattachment. Do not become attached to the material things in this life. He wasn't saying we should not enjoy them, but rather to not become attached. The same lesson is taught in the Bhagavad Gita. Practically every human being is attracted to the shiny, bright object. At least in the West." He paused. "When they obtain it, they show it off to everyone. Then envy strikes. People want what the other person has, and they steal it or get a better version. The moment we glimpse something shinier and brighter than what we have, we become sad. Our toy isn't as good as it was just a moment ago, because there was a brighter and shinier toy. We chase the shiniest object to redeem ourselves, making sure we are better than the other guy or gal. And this is our pursuit of happiness."

"OK, I get it, but that doesn't apply to everyone. I, for example, am not like that. I am at peace with what I have and what I have accomplished."

"Are you really, or are you just settling and accepting the way it is?"

"Uh …" Gary paused, thinking about what Wayne had said. "I never thought about it that way. I guess, in a way, we do settle for things."

"But we don't have to," Wayne emphasized. "Would you like a refresh on your latte?" Wayne asked.

"Yeah, that would be great."

"You got it," Wayne said as he stood up from the table and walked to the counter to order fresh coffee and a latte.

Opposite George

> "O mighty Arjuna, even if you believe the Self to be subject to birth and death, you should not grieve. Death is inevitable for the living; birth is inevitable for the dead. Since these are unavoidable, you should not sorrow."[23] —
> *The Bhagavad Gita*

Egoic Tendencies

Now I Lay Them Down to Rest

Mind

"Listen to this," Wayne exclaimed. He looked at his iPhone and began reading the text on the screen. "'Truth will correct all errors in my mind. I am mistaken when I think I can be hurt in any way. I am God's Son, whose self rests safely in the mind of God.'"[24]

Wayne continued reading, "Here's another one, 'To give and to receive are one in truth. I will forgive all things today, that I may learn how to accept the truth in me, and come to recognize my sinlessness.'"[25]

"What was that? It's not from the Bible," Gary said.

"It's from *A Course in Miracles.*"

"Oh, OK," he replied, not really sure what *A Course in Miracles* was.

"It mentions the mind of God," Wayne commented.

"I wasn't aware that God had a mind." Gary laughed to himself.

"I always believed I had a mind, but after reading that, my understanding of the mind is not what I thought it was."

"How so?"

"What does it mean to have a mind that erroneously believes, or interprets, the world?"

"Uh, I have no clue."

"It seems that I have a mind, and God has a mind as well. So, my question is, is my mind a part of God's mind if my self rests safely in the mind of God?"

"Uh …"

Wayne interrupted, "And then what is self?"

"Uh, I don't know."

"Sin means error. Therefore, sinlessness means without error."

"OK?" Gary responded, not sure where this was headed.

"If we are all born sinners, then we are all born with errors. These errors can be corrected by reconnecting with God, so my errors, or sins, can and will be corrected with truth."

"Uh, sure." Gary replied trying to follow what Wayne was saying.

"So, what is truth?"

"I don't know."

"God is truth, and truth is God. I am a part of God's mind; therefore, I am God. My error is the human error of believing I am separate from God. Although I am separated from God because I am a human being, it does not mean I need to realize separation. This is the error, or the sin. We are all born with error, and the error is our human separation from Source."

"What does separation mean?" Gary asked.

"Apart from. Humans are apart from God, but we are of God; therefore, we are not separate."

"That makes sense, I think."

"We are one but have our own experiences, minds, and thoughts which rest safely in the mind of God. It is all of God, yet we have been given the gifts of free will and choice. It is up to us to choose wisely. So, what is or who is God?" Wayne continued, "Energy, a person, a program? Love is God, and God is Love. So, what is Love? Love is Truth. What is Truth? Truth is Love. The human realm is a realm of duality. If I attempt to remove duality from human experience, I am no longer human. By attempting to remove duality, I am attempting to be God in a human body. But I am in the human form so I can experience this realm which cannot be experienced as pure positive energy or Source alone. This is what I am trying to decipher and challenge. Where we fail and suffer as humans, is not that we enjoy the things of this world, but that we become attached and define our existence based on these things. If we learn to enjoy these things instead of being defined by them and reconnect with God, we will be free."

"OK. I think I follow you."

"Giving and receiving is a cycle. A cycle goes around and around, again and again, repeating itself. Cycle of life, cycle of the seasons. Are they even real or just my interpretation in my mind? And what is mind, then? If I rest safely in the mind of God, then aren't I a part of God? How can I then be separated? What am I separated from?

"The question is, when it comes to the human realm, does it really work? Can I be human and experience the miracles of the human experience while still being one with God, being one with truth?

"All meaning becomes meaningless. The mind is not at all what I have been taught. God is nowhere in the vicinity of what I have been taught or led to believe. It's difficult to accept the truth when it is revealed, because it goes against all we have been told, yet it is up to us to seek and find the truth. Maybe this is why the truth shall set us free?

"My mind is one with God's. But what about the egoic mind that has been led astray to believe in untruth? How do you separate the two? This is separation. Two minds, two realms, two truths. Egoic mind and higher consciousness."

"Uh ..." Gary paused. "You lost me. I need to process what you just said."

Opposite George

> "When you make your mind one-pointed through regular practice of meditation, you will find the supreme glory of the Lord."[26]
>
> — *The Bhagavad Gita*

The Only Constant in Life Is Love

Wayne and Gary were still going strong and highly caffeinated. At this point, they were drinking water to take a break from all of the caffeine. Wayne was rambling off random thoughts. "I saw God for the first time today. I saw all of God's gifts, I saw miracles, I saw life for the first time! I heard all of God's sounds in nature for the first time today!

"Prior to this moment, I saw everything else other than God's gifts and miracles. Each breathing moment is the first time. Today is the first time we will have this exact conversation in this exact place. It will never be experienced again.

"Every moment prior to that, I was running, making sure I did not fall behind. I was 'keeping up with the Joneses,' as they say. And I was great at the chase.

"All the while, during the pursuit, I was keeping my eyes peeled and looking out for danger, avoiding failure and a fear of falling behind. I was doing great, but I missed everything else. I rarely, if ever, enjoyed any of the miracles and gifts I was blessed with.

"It seems we run and run, work hard, and then work harder to get ahead in the hope that one day we can get off the treadmill of life."

Gary sat in silence while Wayne carried on.

"The problem is that all of these pursuits are egoic tendencies, fearful pursuits. They are addictive. We are addicts, always looking for the next high. Afraid to rest and enjoy the moment out of a fear of falling behind. All we really created was a self-defeating pursuit of suffering.

"The moment I rested; it was miraculous. Not only did I not fall behind, but I was also right there in the moment when miracles occur. There was no fear of falling behind and no urgency to get ahead.

"An object in motion tends to stay in motion. Although I stopped the chaotic egoic pursuit, I am still in motion, aligned with Love.

"The answer is love. Love heals all. Love saves all. Heraclitus is known to have said, 'The only constant in life is change.' But, in truth, the only constant in life is Love."

Opposite George

> "Love created me like itself. I am in the likeness of my Creator. I cannot suffer, I cannot experience loss and I cannot die. I am not a body."[27]
>
> — *A Course in Miracles*

What I saw today

I saw someone fall in love for the first time!

I saw a baby enter the world for the first time!

I saw someone make the team for the first time.

I saw someone score a goal for the first time!

I saw someone win a game for the first time.

I saw someone get their first job!

I saw someone make money for the first time.

I heard the birds singing with the morning sunrise for the first time.

I saw someone drive a car for the first time.

I saw someone go to high school for the first time.

I saw someone fly on an airplane for the first time.

I saw someone jump into the ocean for the first time.

I saw someone dig their toes into the sand on the beach for the first time.

I saw gladiators go head-to-head in battle and share a smile.

I was at a Godsmack and Shinedown concert and saw a sea of people together as one.

I saw so many miraculous things today.

Last Words

"When I write my next book, I will write no more," Wayne stated in a matter-of-fact tone.

"Why?" Gary asked in a surprised tone.

"Because the only reason I write is for selfish reasons. To help me break through. I express my fears and frustrations in order to move past them."

"Sure. I see how it must be a cathartic process for you." Gary observed.

"I didn't realize that until I wrote my third and fourth books."

"Was that when you published your children's book and memoir at the same time?"

"Yep. I was doing a book signing when I realized that I enjoy the process of capturing, reflecting, and releasing when I write. But, the troubling part is, when I write I yearn for acceptance and approval of people. That part sucks and is not healthy …"

"Yeah—"

Wayne interrupted, "But, it has also taught me to stop putting so much weight on other people's viewpoints, thoughts, and comments. It is so easy to be afraid if someone does not like what I have to say. And that fear can be paralyzing. I am sure there are countless stories of people who did not move forward with their plans or dreams, or simply didn't speak the truth, out of fear of being ridiculed."

"Well, people find it much easier to bitch, moan, and complain about someone or something rather than pay them a compliment," Gary stated. "It takes the spotlight off of them and casts their fears and doubts on other people. Not everyone, though."

"True. Plus, too many people are like crabs in a bucket."

"What?" Gary asked.

"Ever hear about the analogy of crabs in a bucket? They try to make their escape by climbing to the top of the bucket. The moment one makes it to the top, another crab will latch onto the crab that is making an escape and will pull it back down into the bucket again. They never escape. Humans aren't much different in that regard."

"Hmm." Gary paused. Shaking his head, he mumbled under his breath. "I know people like that." Another pause. "But not everyone—"

Wayne interrupted, "Let me clarify. Because my statement about human behavior was pretty strong. I stand by my comments about humans not being much different than crabs. But this crab behavior is an egoic tendency. We don't want anyone to escape if that means all the rest will be left behind. If one escapes, all of the other crabs want to go as well. If they can't go, then they will pull you back down into their bucket of hell."

"Yep. I was about to say the same thing," Gary commented as he took a sip of his coffee. "Like I was saying, I know plenty of people like that. But I also know many more who are quite the opposite."

"We need to surround ourselves with more people like that. People like you." Wayne floated Gary a compliment. "Although I believe too many people just talk the talk. They might say they are happy about another's success, but deep down, they feel threatened. Especially in sales. Someone might say 'Great job! Congratulations!' But in the same breath they mutter or think something quite the opposite. Secretly, it kills them to see someone who is more successful, wealthier, and so on. They don't want to be left behind." Wayne paused. "Crabs in a bucket."

"I tell people I am happy for them, and I sincerely mean it," Gary firmly stated, to prove he was not a crab as Wayne was portraying.

"You are not a crab, Gary," Wayne interjected. "But you can't deny what I'm saying. Even in your line of work. The pharmaceutical industry is just as corrupt and greedy as financial services. Talk about best interest. The only best interest in pharmaceuticals is profit."

"Dude. Really?" Gary was visibly upset by Wayne's comments. "I love what I do, and my drugs help people!"

"Do they really? Have they cured anyone of their disease yet?"

"Well, uh …" Gary paused. "No, but they help people with their sickness …" Gary was searching for an answer. "It helps them feel better. Uh …" Another pause. "So they can have a better quality of life."

"OK. Fine," Wayne responded. "But, in your heart of hearts, do you really think they cured anything? The multi-billion-dollar business of pharmaceuticals is a fucking Ponzi scheme. They don't cure diseases! You are a fucking snake oil salesman."

"Come on, Wayne. That's not fair. How can you say that?"

"How can I say that? How can you represent that? Especially after the pandemic. The entire thing was a fucking farce. Not once did I or anyone in my family get this so-called virus. No inoculation. No hand-washing. No masks. But people are so afraid and ignorant they will believe anything. The mind is a powerful thing and will manifest your strongest desires or doubts. Fear is a strong emotion. Fear of getting sick. Fear of dying."

"Come on, Wayne. I got sick. My wife had it. My kids all had it."

"Even after being inoculated?" Wayne calmly asked, knowing what Gary's reply would be.

Gary paused. Wayne repeated his question. "Did they get it after being inoculated, Gary?"

"Well, uh …" Gary paused. "Yes, but it could have been much worse if we weren't."

"Gary, I love you. You are a great guy, but you are a fool. Wake up! That's bullshit. You got sick because of the inoculation and because your body needed to cleanse itself. That is what sickness is. That's what symptoms are: the body sending you signs that it's sick and trying to get rid of the toxins that are making it sick." Wayne paused to take a sip of his coffee.

"Listen, the inoculation is what made you sick. Or, because you believed you had something which you didn't. The mind is very powerful. If I seem angry, it's because I am. But really, it's a passion and an intensity of love. Because I see what's going on, and most of the world has been brainwashed. I'm tired of people believing all of this bullshit. They're being led like cattle to slaughter. You do whatever you want, but I care about you and want what's only the best for you. I hope you understand. Remember, you always rattle my cage to make sure I am OK, and you always challenge me, so I am going to do the same for you."

"Well, I know one thing," Gary stated.

"What's that?" Wayne asked.

"I'm definitely not as direct as you are."

"No argument here. Although I am a little sorry if it comes across the wrong way. Sometimes my choice of words aren't the best."

"It's OK. I'm listening. I know you have a better understanding and knowledge of the human body and healing after what Sue went through." Gary paused. "How long has it been?"

"Twenty years."

"Wow! That's amazing. And everything's still good, right?"

"Yes. She's great. She doesn't get sick either. Yes, her body shows signs of being off-balance, every now and then. Like the sniffles, a headache, or feeling stuffed up. She pays attention to the signals from her body and will cleanse her body to rebalance her terrain. Then, miraculously, her symptoms fade, and she's fine. It's pretty awesome and fascinating. The human body is amazing and can heal itself, much more than what we believe." Wayne paused. "That's when I learned the truth about disease and healing. Unfortunately, the medical establishment does a pretty shitty job of curing disease. It's a pretty good money machine, though. They are creating customers for life. People keep coming back year after year for their shots, yet they still get the diseases which the shots are apparently preventing. They take pill after pill on top of pill after pill and get sicker and sicker. The body heals itself, and when you negate the body's natural healing ability with the wrong pills and shots, the body no longer heals. People are so ignorant and afraid, continuing to pop toxic pills and take shots. Then another version of a drug is created, the next best thing on the market, which costs millions of dollars to make. But it still does not cure the disease! Don't you see it?"

"See what?"

"The Ponzi scheme. Like putting a Band-Aid over a gaping wound and saying it heals and cures. All it does is cover up the wound, not cure it. When the Band-Aid no longer works, we just replace it with another Band-Aid. The body heals itself, not the Band-Aid. Fear is powerful. Ignorance is even more powerful. When the two are combined, there is little hope. Diseases are caused by shitty lifestyles, stress, crappy food, toxic air, and water. So the body will always continue to get sick. And until you clean up the shit, the disease will never be cured. What's even more pathetic is that I know the cure for cancer, and no one cares to hear about it. In the end, the majority of people will die from the treatment and not the disease."

"Come on, Wayne! Stop! Do you really believe that?"

"No. I know it. Look, I don't want you or anyone to get sick. But come on! When will people open their eyes?"

"They probably won't." Gary sighed. "I can't fathom what you are saying. But I am listening, and I want to learn, although I still don't fully understand. What you are telling me is not at all what I learned as a kid or in college."

"I know. It took me years to understand this," Wayne stated passionately. "What solidified my understanding and helped me see through the lies was the pandemic. That was the breakthrough for me. It was a miracle of sorts. I escaped the bucket. And the other crabs are not going to pull me back into their bucket of hell. It was difficult and took a long time, but I'm free. I no longer get sick. I can heal. I have healed. Escaping doesn't cost anything except your entire world. When you finally get it and break through, the world you believe in will collapse before your eyes. And that scares the shit out of people. Like you said, it goes against what they were told and taught. Just because it's in a textbook—which happens to be funded by some institution, corporation, or foundation with a shitload of money and an agenda—doesn't make it true. Think about the Thanksgiving holiday. Do you really believe that the white man made peace with the Native Americans? Where are the Native Americans today? They were slaughtered by the white man—kicked off their land and left in a gutter to rot. This happened in the land of the free and brave. A country founded on freedom of speech, freedom of religion, and freedom of belief. Yet they slaughtered the people who were here before them, because the white man did not agree with their beliefs and religion. And don't get me started on slavery."

"Don't worry. I won't." Gary said in relief.

"So what were we talking about before I went off on that tangent?"

"Crabs," Gary commented. "You were talking about people's behavior and how people apparently don't want others to succeed."

"Yep. Thanks! The other thing I was going to say was about when people make snide comments or an arrogant response to a compliment."

"Like what?"

"Have you ever listened to how people speak or interact with one another? Especially kids. And by kids, I am talking first-graders to college students. The instant response to a comment are the following two words ..."

Gary cringed and closed his eyes at what he thought he was about to hear.

Wayne stopped, looked at Gary, and asked, "What are you doing? Why are you making that look?"

"I'm trying to prepare myself for what I'm about to hear." Still cringing, Gary opened one eye, slowly followed by the other eye, and looked at Wayne.

"Really, what do you think I am going to say?"

Gary leaned in and whispered, "Fuck you."

Wayne smiled and chuckled. "Dude. No. That's not what I was going to say. Although I have always been fond of those two words. What I was going to say were the two words that make me want to stand up and punch someone in the face: 'I know.'"

Gary repeated the words with a smile and laughed. "I know. That's the response practically every kid gives. Oh, and by the way, it's not just kids who reply that way. I work with grown adults who act the same way."

"That response should be erased from our vocabulary," Wayne demanded. "It's like crabs pulling all the other crabs back into the bottom of the bucket of hell with them. Think about it. Whenever someone makes a comment or an observation, having to hear the response of 'I know' is symbolic of a crab pulling you down into their bucket of misery. It is such an ignorant and mindless comment. We have become so stupid and fearful that we know nothing." Wayne paused to take a sip of his coffee. "Plus, when my kids or their friends say, 'I know,' I then ask them where they learned to respond like that. Nine out of ten times, their reply is that they learned it from TikTok."

"Oh my gosh, Wayne!" Gary gasped. "Your kids are addicted to TikTok, too?"

"Sadly, yes. What's worse is they also learn this 'I know' response in school. They're becoming fact regurgitators. Like fucking computers. A computer is useless if it does not know what to do with the facts and figures. The computer lacks human emotion and logical reasoning. I keep reminding my kids that it's OK to learn all of the facts and figures, but I also urge them to ask why. How does it apply to life? And how can they use the information to become better? Don't just puke facts and pass a test without asking what it all means and how the information can be used." Wayne continued, "I know so many 'highly intelligent' people who are complete idiots. All they do is regurgitate facts and figures or some bullshit they heard on the news, to prove how smart they are. They're so dumb and don't even realize the computer can regurgitate facts, making them replaceable. Computers are useless without human emotion, logical reasoning, and the simple aspect of being human: loving, caring, and kind."

"I know how you feel about this, Wayne, but I never really understood why you felt that way," Gary commented. "But, the more I think about it and open my eyes to it, I believe you are on to something. Although, in a way, it is quite sad."

"Then there are the assholes who brag about how much money they make. Or the neighborhood they live in. The car they drive. Their vacation. That's the attachment I was talking about. Or they're just arrogant pricks."

"Dude. Hold on. I go on vacation. I enjoy taking breaks and spending time with my family."

"I didn't say *you*, Gary," Wayne retorted with a tinge of annoyance in his voice.

"OK. Just checking."

"You are a good person. Always have been, and always will be. You are patient and kind. You always find the light in everyone, despite their flaws."

"Thanks, Wayne. My wife would say otherwise."

"Well, marriage is another topic. We see it all. The good, the bad, and the ugly. What I've learned is it all depends on what perspective I bring to the relationship." Wayne paused. "The challenge with relationships is we see the other person through our eyes and expectations. So, when a spouse doesn't live up to what's expected of them, or how they believe things should be, they carry it as resentment and frustration. And they often talk to their friends about how annoyed they are with their spouse."

"Yep." Gary shook his head in agreement. "I'm OK with that because men often don't understand women, and vice versa. I believe they talk to their friends because they don't understand male behavior and they really want to."

"I agree, unless it's a bitch session to fuel the fires of frustration and resentment. It's so easy to take all of the good things for granted. And believe me, I know!" Wayne smiled.

"Yeah. It can be too easy to take it for granted. I do my best not to." Gary smiled.

"Well, you are a 'glass is half-full' type of guy. I, on the other hand, am drinking from a half-empty glass. That is what relationships are," Wayne continued. "We tend to focus on differences rather than honoring the positives and the goodness within each of us. An egoic tendency."

"Thanks for the compliment, but I'm not so sure my glass is always half-full. I often get upset and have bad thoughts about colleagues and clients at times."

"I know you do. Everyone does. But you acknowledge it. Acknowledging the frustration and seeking to understand it is great. What you do with it is important, as well. Instead of carrying it with you and trying to find a way to retaliate or get even, you look for ways to become better. You look for ways to work things out, rather than allowing it to fester. There's a big difference! This is all from the ego."

"What do you mean? What's from the ego?" Gary asked.

"When I say 'ego,' I speak of the tendency to feed on fear, greed, envy, revenge, retaliation, hatred, superiority, and so on. Egoic tendencies." Wayne took a sip of his coffee. "I think I need a fresh cup. Can I get you another one?"

"Yeah, that would be great. But can you order mine with an extra shot? The extra caffeine jolt will help with my drive home."

"You got it." Wayne smiled and walked over to the counter to order the drinks.

Opposite George

> "You can speak from the spirit or from the ego, as you choose. If you speak from spirit you have chosen to "Be still and know that I am God." These words are inspired because they reflect knowledge." [28]
>
> — *A Course in Miracles*

Words

While waiting for their drinks, Wayne sat down at the table. "On a different topic, did I show you the picture of my garden?"

"Uh, I don't think so."

"Well, my garden was no longer a garden in the sense of what you would envision a garden to be."

"Why? What kind of garden was it?"

"It was supposed to be a vegetable garden, but it had become more like a jungle!"

"Aah. Was it a weed jungle?"

"Precisely. And it was pretty bad. Take a look at this." Wayne grabbed his iPhone and held it up to his face to unlock it. He opened the photo album and scrolled through all of his pictures. "Hold on. It's in here somewhere."

The barista finished making the drinks and called out Wayne's name. "Wayne! Coffee up! Latte, extra shot up! Drinks up for Wayne."

"I'm going to head to the bathroom while you look for whatever it is you're looking for," Gary said.

"I'm looking for the before and after pictures."

"Of what, the garden?"

"Yep."

"OK."

"Hey, grab my coffee and your latte on your way back."

"Got it." Gary got up from the table.

Wayne scrolled through his iPhone, looking for the pictures. Gary returned from the restroom. He approached the table with their beverages and sat down. "Did you find the pictures?"

"No. I can't find them," Wayne said in frustration. "Ah! I sent them to Sue. I will bring up the text message." Wayne held his iPhone, and with his thumb, he touched the screen at the bottom and swiped his thumb upward toward the top of the screen in a reverse question mark motion. He scrolled through the open apps to find the messages app and tapped it with his thumb. "OK, hold on a sec." He tapped on Sue's name, and then he started swiping with his thumb in a downward motion from top to bottom, scrolling through the messages and looking for the pictures. "Aha! Here they are," Wayne exclaimed. "Take a look at this." He showed Gary the screen. "Do you see that?"

Gary looked at the picture. After a pause, he said, "Whoa, that's your garden?"

"Yep."

"You weren't kidding when you said it was a jungle."

"No shit. But take a look at this." Wayne turned the phone toward himself to open the after picture of the garden. "Take a look." He turned the phone toward Gary.

"Wow! That's impressive. You did all that work?" Gary commented on the picture of the garden.

"Yeah. It was a lot of work, but not as hard as you would think. It was maybe a few hours of work, but it was worth it."

"Nice job."

"Whenever I grabbed a hold of a bunch of weeds and vines, I noticed the scent of mint and lavender with each tug of the weeds. Hidden among the jungle of weeds were mint and lavender plants. And the fresh scents made the weeding experience much more enjoyable."

"Did you save it?" Gary asked.

"Save what? The mint and lavender?"

"Yes."

"Unfortunately, no. I tried to weed around them, but it was too much of a pain in the ass. So I just pulled everything." Wayne paused. "When I finished, I noticed birds arriving to feast on the buffet of seeds and insects that had been unearthed. I love spending time outside, listening to the sounds of nature. It's pretty amazing to hear, see, and smell. Although I'm often easily distracted by my thoughts which often take me away from the moment. Adding to that, hearing the roar of car engines zipping down the road in the distance made me wonder, *is that nature?* I watched the birds flying above the garden. Off in the distance beyond the birds, my view was intercepted by an airplane soaring through the sky leaving a trail of fumes behind it. Is that nature?"

"Are you asking me?"

"Not really. I was asking myself. But think about it. Practically everything man-made is not from nature. It's more like a manipulation of nature. There's no other creature on this planet that can make things the way humans do, by manipulating nature and destroying nature, leaving nasty trails in our wake."

"Uh …" Gary was speechless. "Well …" He was searching for something to say, but the more he thought about what Wayne was saying, the more he realized it was not necessarily wrong.

"I don't want to get into that."

"Really?" Gary responded in surprise.

"Sort of. The birds perched themselves on the wooden fence railing that surrounded the garden and hopped from the fence into the garden to snack on seeds and insects. In that moment, Thich Nhat Hạnh crept into my mind."

"Who? What?" Gary was not sure what Wayne was saying.

"Thich Nhat Hạnh. He was a Vietnamese Buddhist monk, speaker, and author. I recall reading one of his books about Buddhist communities which take care not to cause harm to any living creature. While I was pulling vines and weeds, I wondered if my act of weeding was wreaking havoc, causing harm and destruction for the weeds, the insects, the worms, and other creatures in the garden."

"Well, I think that's an impossible task. You can't avoid causing some form of damage when weeding your garden."

"I agree. Somehow, these Buddhist communities go to great lengths to ensure they do not cause harm to any living creature. I have no idea how they do it, or if it's even possible."

"Yeah, that sounds a little extreme."

"Then a thought crossed my mind. Actually, it was the line from the movie, *The Matrix*: 'There is no spoon.'" Wayne paused.

"Why? What's that have to do with your garden?"

"Nothing, other than the meanings we place on words. There is no spoon," Wayne repeated the popular line from the movie. "There is no weed. Do not try and pull the weed. Instead, try to realize the truth. There is no weed." Wayne humored himself with his play on words from the movie. "Yes! That was it."

"What was it?"

"There are no weeds!" Wayne exclaimed.

"There are no weeds?" Gary replied, slightly confused.

"Why are some plants labeled as weeds, and others are not?"

"Uh, because they're weeds," Gary responded.

"OK, but why are they called weeds?"

"I don't know. Probably because they grow where they aren't supposed to?" Gary responded with a question.

"I really don't know, but I believe that's almost the technical definition of a weed. It grows where it is not supposed to. But according to whom? Who's the one who decided where plants should grow or shouldn't grow?"

"I don't know."

"Is it because they are eyesores on our lawns and gardens? I don't think they are labeled as weeds because they aren't edible. And, as far as nature is concerned, insects, deer, birds, chipmunks, groundhogs, and other creatures consider them food. From an insect's perspective, a weed is food, as well." Wayne continued, "So is a weed really a weed?"

"I don't know?" Gary slowly responded with a question.

"Dandelions!" Wayne blurted abruptly, startling Gary. "What about dandelions? Dandelion wine. Dandelion salad. Dandelion soup. A dandelion is an edible plant, but I have been brainwashed into believing they are bad because they are labeled a weed. This is a perfect analogy for the human experience. We label a thing which it is not because, in most cases, it serves some egoic tendency."

"What?"

"We label things to suit our needs, despite how ludicrous it is or how much harm it might cause. We are conflicted and confused. A weed is not a bad thing. But, because we have labeled it as such, it's now considered a bad thing and an eyesore. The same thing applies to germs, and the farce about viruses and diseases."

"Ugh." Gary sighed.

"Now, I have been led to believe weeds are unsightly. My neighbors certainly think they're unsightly, so much so that they would file a complaint with the police because of my unsightly garden. Hmm. Love thy neighbor … unless they have weeds." Wayne chuckled to himself.

Gary laughed and repeated Wayne's comment, "Love thy neighbor, unless they have weeds."

"Here, listen to this." Wayne picked up his iPhone. He pressed and held the power button and spoke, "What is a weed?"

His phone responded, "Here is what I found."

Wayne read the words displayed on the screen. "'Weed: a weed is a plant considered undesirable in a particular situation, growing where it is not wanted.' There you have it! We label plants as weeds, and now people associate weeds as bad things which must be killed. Dandelions really get a bad rap."

"That's pretty funny."

"Not really," Wayne quickly responded. "Words are intended to communicate, but instead, they segregate. More often than not, words are used as swords to attack, divide, and separate. Despite our best intentions, when using words to communicate and unite, we tend to unknowingly use them to divide. So much so that it has become difficult to recognize truth from falsehood."

Gary sat in silence, taking in what Wayne had just said.

"Use words to define your life, not confine your life," Wayne added. "People try to use big words to sound smart." Wayne lifted his hands, making a gesture in the air to represent big words. "Economy of words. Why can't people talk in normal, everyday words?"

Gary laughed. "That's so true. I work with people who do exactly that. They use big words or fancy words to sound smart. All the while, the person listening knows the person speaking is full of shit."

"Words have no meaning. The moment we put something into words marks the moment all and any meaning is lost. It's now open to interpretation by the speaker of the words and the people who interpret the words. 'Once you label me, you negate me,'" Wayne quoted the theologian and philosopher Søren Kierkegaard.

"Who said that?"

"Søren Kierkegaard. He was a theologian and philosopher from, I believe, around the mid- to late-eighteen hundreds."

Gary repeated the words. "'Once you label me, you negate me.' Hmm. That's interesting."

"How about, 'The Tao that can be told is not the eternal Tao.'"

"I've heard that one before," Gary commented.

"Remember the nursery rhyme, 'Sticks and Stones'?"

"Yep. 'Sticks and stones may break my bones, but words shall never hurt me.'" Gary smiled.

"Sure, sticks and stones may break bones, but words can hurt me, too, if I allow it to happen. Words are a form of energy which can cause more harm, or long-term harm, than a stick or a stone. Hurtful words can be carried for a lifetime, while a broken bone heals and we move on with our lives."

Wayne and Gary grabbed another cup of coffee and a latte to spend the rest of the day enjoying their conversation.

Opposite George

The Tao that can be told is not the eternal Tao.
The name that can be named is not the eternal name.
The nameless is the beginning of heaven and earth.
The named is the mother of ten thousand things.
Ever desireless, one can see the mystery.
Ever desiring, one can see the manifestations.
"These two spring from the same source but differ in name;
this appears as darkness.
Darkness within darkness.
The gate to all mystery."
—*Laozi, Tao Te Ching*

"...it cannot be defined by word or idea; as the Scripture says, it is the One "before whom words recoil."[29]

—*Shankara (*Aldous Huxley, *The Perennial Philosophy)*

"Yet even they will be exchanged at last for what we cannot speak of, for you go from there to where words fail entirely, into a silence where the language is unspoken and yet surely understood."[30]

— *A Course in Miracles*

"Communication, unambiguous and plain as day, remains unlimited for all eternity. And God Himself speaks to His Son, as His Son speaks to Him. Their language has no words, for what They say cannot be symbolized. Their knowledge is direct and wholly shared and wholly one. How far away from this are you who stay bound to this world. And yet how near are you, when you exchange it for the world you want."[31]

— *A Course in Miracles*

Insanity

"Remember Mindlessness Man and the mosh pit of your mind?"

"I do. The moth died chasing the light bulb. You were so lost, you missed your daughter's recital, despite being there in the front row. The mosh pit of the mind is the sixty thousand thoughts a day that go through our minds." Gary smiled.

"Yep! That's it. My mind is an endless loop of insanity." Wayne sighed. "It just replays this loop of angst and anxiety over and over again, like a fucking broken record. It offers no solution. That's the part that I can't deal with. And this is what every human being does, driving them insane."

"Yeah. I guess I do the same thing."

"We all do! It's just that we never pay attention to it. Really, we don't even know it is happening. Sort of like the ringing in my ears."

"What ringing in your ears?"

"My ears constantly ring, twenty-four seven. I never noticed it until I began meditating and sitting in silence. In absolute silence, no meditation music, nothing. The ringing in my ears suddenly became very pronounced. I never knew it was there because I always had some sort of noise piping into my ears. Although I am sure my ears are ringing because of the loud music I played since I was a kid—and continue to play."

"Well, yeah," Gary said sarcastically. "In college, you played your boom box pretty damn loud, and all the time."

"I get it. That was probably what caused the ringing. The loud music. What I was getting at was that we do things we are unaware we are doing. We are even more unconscious to the fact that we can change it."

"OK. True." Gary agreed. "But the hard part is actually making the change."

"Yep. When faced with something challenging or unfamiliar, this loop of anxiety plays continuously in my mind. Even while I'm doing something else or when in a conversation, the loop still plays in the background. But it often pauses when I'm doing something interesting and engaging. But once the activity or conversation ceases, the incessant loop begins again. Like the mosh pit of my mind."

"Yeah, but it's a good thing to play scenarios over again in your head to figure out how to avoid mistakes or improve in the future."

"No doubt. It all depends on what it is that we are playing over and over again. This is the mischievous programming of the mind. We are programmed with fear and anxiety, making us prey of the ego. If we play these anxious thoughts over and over again with no resolutions or answers, we end up being the victims of the fear-based chatter which has been implanted in our minds. I don't know the solution, other than changing the loop of anxiety and fear permanently." Wayne passionately spoke.

"Yeah, but that's the fight-or-flight response system which is intended to be a survival tactic."

"Thank you for saying that. I call bullshit, though. It is not a life-or-death thing. It is social anxiety. The brain has been tricked into believing almost everything is a fight-or-flight scenario. Just watch the news, any movie, or a Netflix series. It is all about fear, anxiety, and death. It's rather simple to change. When I change the loop to love, happiness, and all things good, the entire world changes right before my eyes. Listen to this for a moment." Wayne grabbed his iPhone and scrolled to find a quote saved in his notes. "OK, here it is." Wayne began reading. "'It is as if a circle held it fast, wherein another circle bound it and another one in that, until escape no longer can be hoped for nor obtained. Attack, defense; defense, attack, become the circles of the hours and the days that bind the mind in heavy bands of steel with iron overlaid, returning but to start again. There seems to be no break nor ending in the ever-tightening grip of the imprisonment upon the mind.'[32]

"That is our insanity, and we have no clue," Wayne continued. "We are all insane, doing the same routines over and over again every day, believing we are sane and that something different is going to happen. We are all puppets. You've heard the following saying, 'the definition of insanity is doing the same thing over and over again, expecting a different result.'"

"Oh yeah! That's one of our favorite sayings in sales. Especially when things don't seem to be working, and we keep using the same sales approach, activity, and metrics."

"This aptly captures human behavior. We are all insane and habitual creatures."

"Why would you say that?"

"Think about it. Just step back and observe the behavior of people. You will see it is pretty clear we are insane."

"How so?"

"We do the same damn things over and over again, every day of our lives, expecting something different or some sort of miracle to save us. We live our lives like Phil Connors in the movie *Groundhog Day* starring Bill Murray." Wayne grabbed his iPhone and typed "Groundhog Day movie" into the browser and read the description. "Listen. 'He discovers that it's Groundhog Day again, and again, and again ... then comes the realization that he is doomed to spend the rest of eternity in the same place, seeing the same people do the same thing every day.'[33]

"We wake up. Brush our teeth, go to the bathroom, bathe, get dressed, grab a cup of coffee, maybe eat breakfast, and go to work or school. Then we come home, eat, watch TV or binge on Netflix or TikTok, check social media, go to the bathroom, brush our teeth, and go to bed. We may do other things in between, like playing sports, going to the bar, dancing, having sex, or whatever. Either way, it's the same damn thing every single day of our lies."

"You meant to say every day of our lives, right?" Gary asked.

"Nope. I meant to say 'lies.' Our lives are really lies. You live a lie. I live a lie. Well, not any longer. We each live a lie. Stings a bit, doesn't it?"

"Yeah. You're being a little bit of an asshole, don't you think?" Gary replied, annoyed by Wayne's comments.

"Why?"

"My life is not a lie. I love my wife. I love my kids. I am happy to have a friend like you in my life. I love my job. How can you say that?" Gary retorted.

"It's hard to hear. The immediate response is to deny it, to prove it wrong or to dismiss what you just heard. But you will replay those words over and over again in your head. Maybe it would be better to restate it as an illusion or a dream. Chasing success is a lie. Chasing money is a lie. Paying taxes is a crime. Yet we all do it without a second thought, over and over again, expecting lives of ease and freedom. You spend your lie chasing, and then you die, leaving behind everything you chased, took pride in, and identified yourself with. Live a lie, and then you die. You know it's a lie when you understand we don't die. This is why we are slaves. We are born, and we enter the world as prisoners and slaves."

"Dude, come on. What are you saying?" Gary responded more annoyed than before. "How can you say life is a lie and we are slaves?"

"Because, Gary, we are! Pay attention. Look at all of the college graduates who do not pursue careers based on what they majored in. Who really knows at the age of eighteen who they are going to be for the rest of their lives? Yet we pressure kids into deciding the rest of their lives at eighteen. And that decision is based on their parents' expectations of themselves, not of their children. We don't have to be slaves, but we will never realize that we are until we open our eyes. This is what life is; from freedom we depart to enter the world as prisoners and slaves. We come from Source, Holy Spirit, or whichever term you prefer, and we are imprisoned by our bodies."

"OK, please explain," Gary interjected.

"Then we are enslaved by our laws, rules, and taxes. We are never free until we awaken, or we leave our prison cells and return to Source. The need to control others is an exercise in futility. It will never work. Even if we control someone, we become the prisoner who will never be free, because we have to always guard the prison cell. The warden becomes the prisoner. We are prisoners in our own bodies, yet we can be free in any moment."

"Well, we need laws and rules to keep peace."

"Do we really, Gary?"

"Yeah," Gary replied in a less than convincing tone.

"I also believe rules and laws are intended to keep the peace. But there is a point at which it strays from keeping peace. When this happens, the rules and laws are no longer used to keep the peace; instead, they are used to control people."

"Uh, I see your point, but I don't think I fully agree. It would be chaos if there weren't any rules and laws. But regretfully, I also see a shift toward using them to control society. Especially in the past few years."

"In the last few years, the pendulum has really swung in the other direction, and it's pretty damn clear the rules and laws are being used to control and imprison people. When someone wants to control and rule people, they imprison—or enslave—them. It is just a matter of making the choice to awaken to higher consciousness. This change of perspective will change our experience of life for the better."

"Dude, you always amaze me and take things to another level." Gary smiled, shaking his head. "I will have to process all of this. You definitely gave me something else to think about."

"Well, you know I take things to the extreme. I am seeking truth, understanding, and meaning. And my choice of words may not always be the best. If I come across as being angry, it is really an intensity of love and wanting to understand what it all means."

"Oh, don't worry. I know you do, and that's what is so great about our conversations. You always give me a different perspective."

"I love and appreciate life more every day because I see through the lie. I love my life because the lie has opened my eyes to life. The reason people feel miserable, stressed, or anxious is because they live a lie and are not living life."

Opposite George

> "Because personality is a process, the human being is constantly remaking himself or herself. Left to itself, the mind goes on repeating the same old habitual patterns of personality. By training the mind, however, anyone can learn to step in and change old ways of thinking; that is the central principle of yoga."[34]
>
> — *The Bhagavad Gita*

> "Reshape yourself through the power of your will; never let yourself be degraded by self-will. The will is the only friend of the Self, and the will is the only enemy of the Self."
>
> "To those who have conquered themselves, the will is a friend. But it is the enemy of those who have not found the Self within them."[35]
>
> — *The Bhagavad Gita*

"Every symptom the ego makes involves a contradiction in terms, because the mind is split between the ego and the Holy Spirit, so that whatever the ego makes is incomplete and contradictory."[36]

— *A Course in Miracles*

"Love Created Me Like Itself. I am in the likeness of my Creator. I cannot suffer, I cannot experience loss and I cannot die. I am not a body."[37]

— *A Course in Miracles*

"I give you to the Holy Spirit as part of myself. I know that you will be released, unless I want to use you to imprison myself. In the name of my freedom I choose your release, because I recognize that we will be released together."[38]

— *A Course in Miracles*

Ask Not to Be Forgiven

"Why do people continually go to confessional?"

"Because they are seeking forgiveness for their sins," Gary replied.

"Well, that's silly." Wayne chuckled.

"Why?"

"Because I am not sure it works. It's sort of like a child who is misbehaving and saying they are sorry. They learn nothing and end up misbehaving again and again."

"Well, that is why people go to confessional, to repent."

"You mean to apologize and ask for forgiveness."

"If you say so." Gary sighed.

"Again, that is just stupid. How about being aware of the behavior, and understanding why they behaved the way they did, and then begin to correct the behavior so they no longer misbehave or sin?"

"I don't know."

"Could it be because they truly have not forgiven themselves for their 'sins'?" Wayne raised his hands, gesturing air quotes. "We may ask for forgiveness over and over again, but if we cannot forgive ourselves by truly accepting and loving ourselves, we may never achieve forgiveness."

"So the only way to forgive is by forgiving yourself first?"

"Yep! The moment you forgive yourself, love yourself, and accept yourself, there will be no need to forgive anyone. The need for attack vanishes from your existence."

"That makes sense, but it seems too simple."

"It is simple, but very difficult to do. Unraveling our egoic tendencies, our past and attachments, is the difficult part. We only attack, feel attacked, or say we should forgive another, if we believe we are attacked or can be attacked. Here's an affirmation I recite daily: 'Safety is the complete relinquishment of attack.'"[39]

"So are you saying people should stop forgiving if they still carry hate, hurt, and resentment?" Gary questioned Wayne.

"That's part of it. Think about it. Love does not hold us hostage. But the ego does. That's the ego's purpose. To hate and seek revenge. To create fear through attachment and identification with the transient things of this world. Therefore, the thought of losing things and our identities scares us to death. And we will do anything to cheat death.

"Love from higher consciousness does not need to fight. It does not honor fear or have knowledge of its existence. Love simply is. It is flow. Like the Tao or Brahma. Love does not need to fight in order to exist.

"On the other hand," Wayne continued. "The ego fights, is selfish, and seeks revenge. If we experience suffering or pain, whether it is our own, a loved one's or a friend's, if someone is treated poorly, hurt by another, or even offended, the immediate response is to attack, defend, and seek revenge. Maybe even kill or go to war. This is the ego. These reactions and feelings certainly do not emanate from love.

"When someone says they are seeking revenge because someone they love was hurt, this is an egoic tendency. It is only the ego that seeks revenge. When you explore the idea of forgiveness even further, it is the ego that says we must forgive. God knows not of forgiveness, because in order to forgive, we must acknowledge hurt, which is of the ego and fear. God is not the ego and is not fear."

Without taking a breath, Wayne continued. "Plus, when you explore it further, forgiveness is an egoic tendency as well. Someone who is aligned with higher consciousness does not seek forgiveness or say we should forgive one another, because hurt, attack, and revenge do not manifest in one who is aligned with higher consciousness."

"Are you saying it does not exist? That they don't experience attack or hate?" Gary asked.

"That's exactly what I am saying. These egoic tendencies are nonexistent in the realm of higher consciousness. Forgiveness is unknown because there is nothing to forgive. Listen to this line from *A Course in Miracles*." Wayne held his iPhone up to his face to unlock it. He swiped his fingertip from right to left and tapped the upper right-hand corner of the screen. He then swiped the screen with his finger in an upward motion a couple times. "OK, here it is." He began to read.

"'No one forgives unless he has believed in sin, and believes that he still has much that needs to be forgiven.'"[25] Oh yeah. Let's look at the Bible verse, 'And Jesus said, 'Father, forgive them, for they know not what they do.''[26] Jesus loved. Jesus was the Messiah. He took on suffering. He did not need to, yet he did. So why would Jesus ask us to be forgiven?"

"Because we are born sinners. He was asking for God's forgiveness," Gary replied.

"But why didn't Jesus say, 'I forgive you brothers, for you know not what you do' instead of, 'Father, forgive them, for they know not what they do.'"

"I don't know. I haven't thought about that."

"He asked for His Father's forgiveness because, despite his efforts, Jesus knew he could not save us." Wayne paused. "But wasn't he the Messiah?"

"Yes."

"Didn't he perform miracles?"

"Yes."

"So what if Jesus could not find it within himself to forgive us?"

"What are you saying?"

"After the horrific torture and beating which led to his death, how could anyone find it within themselves to forgive such tragic, criminal, and horrific actions?"

"Are you sure you want to go down that path?" Gary asked in a concerned tone.

"Why?"

"Because." Gary paused. "Because you shouldn't."

"Why?"

"It's just something that should not be discussed."

"Why?"

"Because we should not speak ill of Jesus or God."

"Really? I'm not talking ill of God nor Jesus. Am I?"

"Uh, no."

"So why is it taboo to talk about it? Especially if I am seeking understanding."

"Because it just is."

"Well, that gives me more cause and curiosity to explore it. Because we aren't 'supposed to' is not a good reason. It's like someone is hiding something or afraid to reveal the truth."

"OK, explore away," Gary said, not wanting to argue. Plus, deep down, he was curious to hear what Wayne would uncover.

"Thanks. I will. What if Jesus could not find it within himself to forgive us? Maybe that is why he asked God for forgiveness," Wayne stated.

"It certainly is an eye-opener and quite humbling. It makes you think about what we did to the Son of God," Gary said candidly.

"Forgiveness is known only to man, but it is also a tool to open our hearts and minds to the path of Love. The moment of our awakening marks the end of forgiveness, because there will be no need to forgive since there will be no evil deeds."

"I am having a difficult time hearing this. But I am intrigued, so please go on."

"Maybe Jesus knew the ego could be outwitted. The ego strikes fear in humans. Could it be that it is the ego that says we should forgive, because as long as we believe in hatred and revenge, the ego uses forgiveness as a ploy? The ego knows we will seek revenge and hold resentment, despite our words saying that we 'forgive someone.' Then it hauls out our past sins, using them to attack us and remind us of our errors. And, making it worse, the ego is so powerful that, although it goes along with the forgiveness narrative, it sinks its claws in deep. We find it nearly impossible to forgive despite our well-intended words, because it is the ego which makes us feel weak and vulnerable. Leading us to believe our brothers are getting away with their transgressions or trespasses.

"When we get little glimpses of higher consciousness, the ego tries to pull us back into its hell. It scares the shit out of us, making us believe we will die or we will lose our identities. The ego makes it seem unfathomable to envision life without labels, things, designations, status, and attachments. We are crabs in a bucket."

"Hey, what do you think about this?" Gary posed a question to Wayne.

"What's that?" Wayne asked.

"The mosh pit of your mind!"

"What about it?" Wayne asked eagerly.

"The crabs are the negative thoughts in the mosh pit of your mind. As you explained, it seems nearly impossible to escape a mosh pit. Our negative thoughts keep us in the mosh pit, and we can't seem to escape. The crabs are the thoughts that we have been fed and led to believe in, preventing us from escaping. The moment we change our mind, the crabs will no longer pull us down into a bucket of hell. Instead, they will allow us to rise up, escape the bucket, and achieve higher awareness."

"Holy shit, Gary! I love that!" Wayne paused to contemplate what Gary had just said. "We can escape the bucket and achieve higher awareness the moment we change our thoughts about ourselves, the world, and the people in it."

It was getting a little late in the day, and Gary needed to begin his trek back home, which was an hour drive away. "I've got to get going soon. Bella is planning dinner, so I should get going soon. I'm going to hit the bathroom and then head home."

"OK. I am glad we had a chance to finally sit down, face to face, and talk. Thank you."

"Anytime, Wayne. I love hearing your perspective of things. I will always keep an open mind. And, although I may not agree with everything, I always listen."

"Thanks, Gary. Thank you for your friendship and for always listening."

"Of course," Gary replied as they walked out the front door of the coffee shop.

Opposite George

"Ask not to be forgiven, for this has already been accomplished. Ask, rather, to learn how to forgive, and to restore what always was to your unforgiving mind."[40]
— *A Course in Miracles*

"Do not try and bend the spoon. That's impossible. Instead, only try to realize the truth. There is no spoon. Then you will see that it is not the spoon that bends. It is only yourself."[41]
— *The Matrix*

"In the holy instant it is understood that the past is gone, and with its passing the drive for vengeance has been uprooted and has disappeared. The stillness and the peace of *now* enfold you in perfect gentleness. Everything is gone except the truth."[42]
— *A Course in Miracles*

"There is an infinite changeless reality beneath the world of change. This same reality lies at the core of every human personality. The purpose of life is to discover this life experientially; that is to realize God while here on earth."[43]
—*The Bhagavad Gita, The Perennial Philosophy*

"Some of the Pharisees asked Jesus, "When will the kingdom of God come?" Jesus answered, "God's kingdom is coming, but not in a way that you will be able to see with your eyes. People will not say, 'Look, here it is!' or, 'There it is!' because God's kingdom is within you."[44]
—*Luke 17:20–21*

"You are indeed afraid to look within and see the sin you think is there. This you would not be fearful to admit. Fear in association with sin the ego deems quite appropriate, and smiles approvingly. It has no fear to let you feel ashamed. It doubts not your belief and faith in sin."[45]
—*A Course in Miracles*

"What if you looked within and saw no sin? This "fearful" question is one the ego never asks. And you who ask it now are threatening the ego's whole defensive system too seriously for it to bother to pretend it is your friend."[46]
—*A Course in Miracles*

"Miracle-minded forgiveness is only correction. It has no element of judgment at all. The statement "Father forgive them for they know not what they do" in no way evaluates what they do. It is an appeal to God to heal their minds. There is no reference to the outcome of the error. That does not matter."[47]
—*A Course in Miracles*

"No one forgives unless he has believed in sin, and still believes that he has much to be forgiven. Forgiveness thus becomes the means by which he learns he has done nothing to forgive. Forgiveness always rests upon the one who offers it, until he sees himself as needing it no more." [48]
—*A Course in Miracles*

"There is nothing to forgive. No one can hurt the Son of God." [49]
—*A Course in Miracles*

"And Jesus said, "Father, forgive them, for they know not what they do." And they cast lots to divide his garments." [50]
—*Luke 23:34*

I can forgive all things today because giving and receiving are one in truth.

Kill or Heal

It was a Tuesday morning. Travis, the exterminator, stopped by the house for his monthly visit to check for pests. Upon completing his inspection of the house, Wayne stepped out of the office to say hello. He enjoyed chatting with Travis, usually spending ten to fifteen minutes talking about the world, family, and life.

"Hey, Travis. Thanks for the ant bait the last time you were here."

"No problem. Did it work? You should have seen a swarm of ants around the bait."

"Oh yeah!" Wayne exclaimed. "I didn't know what it was when I found it. I thought one of my kids was doing a school project or had cut a drinking straw into little pieces. When I found the piece of straw surrounded by ants, I realized it was filled with bait, so I left it alone."

"Good. I'm glad you didn't move it. Let me know if you need more."

"I will. Thanks, Travis."

"They just eat it, not knowing it will kill them," Travis said. "Ants find food, sugar and protein, eat it, and take it back to the colony to feed and nourish the entire colony. Unbeknownst to them, they are being poisoned, and the very food they provide for the other ants will kill the entire colony."

"That's so strange, and in a way, it's sort of sad."

"Yeah, but this could happen to me!" he observed. "I see a cupcake, and I eat it. It could be filled with poison, and like the ant, I could die. They just go about their day, eating the food that is provided for the colony, completely unaware they are being poisoned."

"Yep. Humans aren't much different. Humans constantly eat food which slowly poisons the body. Their shitty diets lead to cancer, heart disease, diabetes, and so on. You name the disease, and we've caused it. Even worse, people believe they are being healed with pills and medications prescribed by their doctors; but in truth, they are being poisoned, exterminated like ants."

"We are victims of convenience," Travis added.

"Yep. If you want to kill something, you fight it and attack it. If you want to heal something, you love it," Wayne stated. "It seems, in our world, we have it backward. The way we cure disease is to treat disease with disease. Attack and destroy in order to heal. And, in order to love and find peace, we must first hate. We go to war and kill in order to have peace. Doesn't make sense, does it?"

"Now that you put it that way, that sounds insane!"

"If you were to say that you were going to kill someone so you could be happy and have peace, you would be called a kook and would be locked up!"

"Yep, sure would." Travis chuckled.

"But it's OK to go to war and kill in the name of peace. We go to war and kill in order to create peace. What's truly insane is that practically everyone on the planet believes it and readily accepts it as though it is perfectly normal. I mean, we glorify war so damn much."

"You know, I think you're right, and I love watching war movies."

"Do you remember the movie, *Apocalypse Now*?" Wayne asked.

"Of course!" Travis exclaimed. "'I love the smell of napalm in the morning. The smell. You know that gasoline smell. It smells like victory.'"

"How about this quote? 'We train young men to drop fire on people, but their commanders won't allow them to write 'Fuck' in their airplanes because it's obscene!'"

"Did Colonel Kurtz say that?"

"Yep. You should read the book, *On Killing.* Humans are not killing machines but are trained to kill. It is not a normal behavior, yet video games are used to train people to become killing machines."

"I will have to check it out," Travis commented.

"Yeah. It's a good book. But I digress. What I was getting at is that the same thing applies to healing and curing disease. If I told you I was going to treat your cancer with a treatment that causes cancer and can kill you, you would call me a kook! Or, if someone told you they were going to inject your body with the very disease that is making you sick in order to cure you of the disease, you would tell them they were insane! Let me ask you this, if you were to start a fire with gasoline and wanted to put the fire out, would you pour gasoline on the fire?"

"Well, of course not. That would be stupid!"

"Exactly, but this is what nearly every human being on the planet does when it comes to curing disease. They do it without batting an eye. Because someone in a white lab coat with designations after their name said it was the only way. Really? People need to stop giving their power away!"

"I agree. But I wouldn't know where to begin."

"Well, it begins with conversations like these. There are thousands of other people who see through the lies, but we cannot just come out and say it. Therefore, we remain inconspicuous."

"Yeah, that makes sense. It's sad that people who know the truth and truly want to help have to remain hidden."

"Or killed. Nearly everything we have been told about life from the mass media, Hollywood, and even the educational system is a fabrication. For example, if you want to stop war in order to have peace, you must go to war. In order to stop killing, you must kill those who kill. If you want to become immune to the flu, you must attack your body with the flu. Yet, every year, hundreds of thousands of people die from the flu despite being inoculated, which is intended to prevent the flu."

"Oh. Really?"

"Yep. Without a doubt! Influenza is the 'I eat too much shit disease!'"

"I never really thought about it."

"Well, it doesn't make any sense. If you have cancer, they will attack and remove the cancer. Afterward, they will inject your body full of cancer-causing chemicals. These chemicals will destroy any remaining cancer and will apparently heal you. But what about the healthy parts of the body? Won't the treatment kill those cells and damage healthy parts of the body?" Wayne paused.

"Doesn't it just kill the cancer?"

"Not only the cancer, Travis. It goes into the entire blood system. That is why people get so sick, lose weight, and their hair falls out. Even infertility, early onset menopause and on and on. Cancer cells are diseased cells which were once healthy, but now they are in a weakened state. Exposed to chemicals, they will die before the healthy cells die. But it comes with a price. The healthy cells are also exposed and therefore weakened and possibly killed. It attacks the entire human body and immune system."

"Oh, wow! Really?"

"Yep. I gave you a very general version, but you get the point. Have you ever noticed that prescription drugs and most treatments come with side effects?

"Yeah. Every commercial on TV, half of the commercial is about all of the side effects."

"That's not healing, but just covering up and creating another ailment," Wayne continued. "After that's complete, they will radiate your body to annihilate any remaining traces of the cancer, despite being fully aware that radiation causes cancer. At that point, the doctors say something like, 'We believe we got it and removed the cancer. So you should be OK.' They 'believe' they got all of the cancer. And the patient 'should' be OK. Seriously? And for the rest of your life, you are looking over your shoulder for it to come back. Checking in with the doctor twice a year for a scan to see if the cancer returned. That's ass-backward, too! Why aren't people going back to see how healthy the body is, rather than checking to see if the cancer returned? That's fucking depressing. And stress is a trigger for cancer. That doesn't sound like a cure, does it?"

"Uh, not really."

"Of course, God forbid it comes back. And when it does come back, they will have to take even more extreme measures to attack and destroy the cancer again, beating the shit out of your body and immune system, making it even harder to recover. Then, as far as quality of life is concerned, good luck. It's no fun looking over your shoulder for the rest of your life, afraid the disease will come back after the doctors apparently got it all and 'cured' you. Sorry, but they didn't cure you. It was more like a Band-Aid placed over an open wound. It might work for a while, but it will not heal, and eventually, the wound will become infected." Wayne paused to take a sip of water from his water bottle. He was on a roll and continued speaking. "In order to love, you must first hate. The more you hate, the more you will heal and find love. How about we just don't hate in the first place, and we can avoid the drama?"

Travis was speechless. "I am glad I spoke with you today. Thanks."

"Sorry if I was a little over the top, but this is important, and people need to take their power back."

"No problem. Thank you for sharing. I have a few friends you should meet."

"Great. I love speaking with like-minded people. By the way, here's what's going to happen. People will become tired of watching their loved ones grow old, get sick, suffer, and die unnatural deaths. Or, they will grow tired of seeing their loved ones get sick, suffer, and die early and unnatural deaths. They will grow tired of seeing people suffer from diseases which could have been prevented. They will grow tired of seeing loved ones suffer and die from the treatments rather than the diseases. They will become sick and tired.[51]

"It's about time we end this suffering and no longer give away our power to someone in a white coat who has been trained to diagnose, cut, remove and attack rather than heal. We will awaken to the truth and the real healing power of love, which is good food, clean air, clean water, and a positive mindset and belief system. Each of us holds the key to a cure the moment we take back our power. Not through some cutting-edge technology or treatment. It will be through the awakening of human consciousness and alignment with love. We are the cause, and we are the cure. Sometimes we have to walk through the stages of hell in order to be saved. Personally, it took me many years of research to understand this. What proved to be most difficult was breaking free from what everyone has been taught and believes about the disease and the cure."

"I'm going to share this with my wife. She would love talking with you."

"Anytime. I'm here to help. I have been ridiculed, criticized, and even hated. I even saw people lose their lives to a treatment, rather than to the disease itself. I have been blessed to see the light of true healing. Sure, I have lost relationships along the way, but I have gained so much more."

"Really?"

"Oh yeah, especially with the farce of a pandemic. That was certainly a moment of truth, and I lost plenty of friendships. But I have found new friendships, as well. My journey will continue. It just won't be through the valley of disease and death. But, for those who remain lost and misguided, this journey of sharing, healing, and curing will remain. Pain is a wrong perspective. Ever since my wife's diagnosis with stage-four cancer twenty years ago, we have learned to no longer fear disease. But rather, embrace health and healing. Fear is a very powerful emotion; it changes our perspective of the world. It can cause disease, it can cause us to behave in ways and do things we would not do under normal circumstances. The moment we change our perspective from fear and pain to one of love and peace, our entire existence changes for the better," Wayne paused. "Plus, I no longer get sick."

"Excuse me? I didn't catch that," Travis replied.

"I said I don't get sick."

"Really? How? That's not possible."

"First of all, 'sick' is just a label with so many different meanings. My body becomes imbalanced, and when it does, I restore the harmony of my body."

"What does that mean?" Travis asked out of curiosity.

"Well, the body is a living miracle of health and healing. But, in order to remain vital and energetic, it must maintain a healthy balance. If I eat too much of the wrong thing, drink too much of the wrong thing, or am stressed and feed my mind with too many bad thoughts, my body will let me know. And when it does, I pay attention to the signs and restore balance. And water is at the core of remedy. Clean, purified, alkaline water. Four liters each day is the key. Three is not enough. Seven or more is a cure. Simple as that.

"I have not been sick in over ten years, ever since I began drinking four to five liters of filtered, alkaline water each day, and by changing my lifestyle. Yes, I feel the signs from my body at times, but I remedy them with water and sweat, which is usually a sauna. Simple as that. My wife hasn't been sick a single day since her diagnosis with stage-four cancer twenty years ago."

"No shit!" Travis gasped.

"Yep, it's pretty amazing. We are blessed that we had the greatest doctor anyone could ask for. And because of what we learned about disease, the body, and real healing, I will not get sick or die of a disease. Now, I do confess that it could happen because of my thoughts. I carried a great amount of anger throughout my life experience, so if I don't cleanse my mind and align my thoughts, this is what will be the cause of any sickness if it were to arise. I really don't care, though. I will decide whether or not I want to remain here and carry on. If I do, then I will heal."

"Wayne, I am inspired by your wife's story, her strength, and her fortitude. I never realized how much you guys had your finger on the magic of life."[52]

"I will leave you with this. I have not been inoculated since I was a kid. Maybe once for the flu over fifteen years ago or so; other than that, I haven't had any inoculations other than when I was a child."

"Seriously? You haven't gotten the flu shot?"

"Nope! And do you know what? When I did, that was when I was the sickest. I remember as a kid being violently ill on a number of occasions. I remember it to this day. In addition to that, I typically would get extremely sick once or twice a year. And you know why?" Wayne asked, immediately answering his question. "Because I believed the bullshit that cold bugs and flu bugs magically appeared every winter and were floating around waiting to attack me. I would fucking get sick! Now that I know it's a bunch of bullshit, I no longer get sick each year. It was mind induced and stress-induced. Plus, my shitty diet and lifestyle didn't help things. The combination of learning about the body and real healing, along with my wonderful life coach, is what cured me of this biannual cycle of getting extremely sick. Before then, I believed in it so much that I would get sick around the same time every year."

Travis stood there, intently listening to Wayne.

"After all those years, I have changed my mind, my diet, and my lifestyle, and I no longer get sick. The cure is at our fingertips: clean water, clean food, and clean minds. Whenever my body displays signs of being out of balance, I listen to the signs and realign with water."

"Well, I have to get to my next appointment. Always enjoy chatting with you. I will see you next time."

"Sounds good. Thanks, Travis. Be well."

Opposite George

"I choose the joy of God instead of pain. Pain is a wrong perspective."[53]
— *A Course in Miracles*

"Those who are healed become the instruments of healing."[54]
— *A Course in Miracles*

The germ is nothing. The terrain is everything.
Antoine Béchamp was right.

Your Happiness Will Never Be Found in Someone Else

It was a beautiful weekend. Wayne was enjoying the day with his oldest daughter. The air was crisp and whispered hints of spring. They walked through the parking lot of the Lawrence Park Shopping Center, talking about school and her softball team. She was out of sorts, and Wayne could sense a tinge of frustration in her energy and words. There were so many similarities between him and his daughter. When she was out of sorts, he felt her energy, which affected him. He did his best not to cast his past life experiences into his daughter's present. But whenever she was upset, or expressed doubt, it triggered his own doubt and fear which he still wrestled with. His frustration was his irrational fear that his daughter would experience the same doubt and fear he'd experienced. He also realized it was selfish and unfair to cast his fears upon her by believing she would go down the same path as he did. As a parent, he does what most parents do by trying to save and protect their child.

Wayne believed this was the best approach, but it was also shortsighted. He was aware that he was being unfair to his daughter by casting his experience upon her, so he did his best to explain the way he acted and reacted to things. It was all based on his past experience and perception of the world, which was not her experience or perception of the world. After many years of introspection, when he felt an egoic response boiling up, he did his best to avert it. Nowadays, he would rarely fall for the ego's allure. There were still times when he got sucked in and reacted with fear, frustration, and anger. But, after the storm clouds created by the egoic mind cleared up, he explained to his daughter how and why he'd acted and reacted the way he did.

"Happiness comes from within rather than without. Stop searching for the answer in other people. Find it within yourself."

"What, Dad?"

"The moment you accept and love yourself is the moment you find true happiness. This is when you own your happiness, which is eternal and cannot be taken."

"Huh?"

"What I mean is, do not look for everyone's approval to validate who you are. Your happiness will not come in the form of someone's approval. Not even mine. It will not come in the form of your grades. It will not come in the form of money. It will not come in the form of status. All of these things are worthy goals and excellent achievements, but they will not be the answer to real happiness."

"Sure. Whatever."

"Yes, they are good, and they contribute to your well-being, but they are not what ultimately create honest-to-goodness happiness. This comes from within. We are brought up to believe that money buys us happiness. It seems as though it does, but there are always strings attached. Sure, it will bring you immediate satisfaction and happiness, but it will quickly wear off. Then you end up chasing your happiness in the form of the next shiny object. It will never end." Wayne paused. "So, if you are able to realize your happiness within yourself, by loving and accepting who you are, you will flip the script and reveal true happiness. The ego will tell you otherwise. The ego will deny it and make you fight to defend it and protect it."

"OK, Dad. Why are you telling me this?"

"Uh, I really don't know. I guess I am trying to explain how to enjoy everything you do and achieve in life, but to not become attached and base your identity on them. They are transient and will not last forever. The moment they are gone, broken, or taken away, you will be lost, maybe feel deep sadness or whatever emotion floods your head. Your true happiness is eternal."

"OK. I'll do my best."

"What if you make a bad play on the field? What if your coach yells at you? What if you break up with your boyfriend? What if you fail a test?"

"Uh, I don't know, Dad. I never thought about it."

"Well, I guess that's a good thing. That tells me you are in the moment versus worrying about what was or what could be."

"Dad! What are you talking about?" She rolled her eyes.

"If you learn from the differences in others to become better, rather than comparing yourself, life will be much more fulfilling. Comparing yourself to others is a never-ending spiral of misery, and then things will suck!"

"That sounds stupid. I'm not sure what you are saying, Dad."

"I am trying to help you avoid the anxiety and stress practically everyone else goes through."

"Thanks, Dad, but I am not you."

"Good point. I apologize. I am simply trying to help you avoid the mistakes I made."

"What if you are wrong?"

"Listen, I carried a lot of anger for a long time."

"Carried? Are you sure you still don't carry anger?"

"Ha. Funny. Don't be a smart-ass." Wayne chuckled. "Anger provides an immediate feeling of strength and power, but it is not everlasting. The momentary rush of seeming strength and power quickly fades, leaving you chasing more. Like an addict."

"OK. I'm still not really sure what you are saying."

"So what if true strength and enduring power reside in love and kindness? And what if the dynamic of fear is wrong?"

She chuckled. "I still don't know what you are talking about, but you are out of your mind if you think I'm going to be lovey-dovey with everyone. Have you been to my school? You've been to my softball tournaments! There is no lovey-dovey Mister Nice Guy there."

"OK, I understand. But maybe this is something that will benefit you when you are older. Maybe it can benefit you now. Who knows?"

"I sure don't." She sighed, rolling her eyes again.

"Well, just imagine for a second ... what if the jerks, the hurtful things people say and do, were replaced with true and honest kindness? What would that mean about the world you live in and experience?"

"Not possible. So I won't imagine it. I can't even try!" she responded.

"Think about tennis and softball. Imagine finding your strength, competing, winning, and dominating from a place of love. An intensity of love, not from a hateful or war mindset."

"Dad, sometimes you worry me with all of this mind talk."

"No need to be worried, just be curious. Without hate, war, and a need for domination, the ego has no purpose. In our entire existence as human beings, there doesn't seem to have been a point in time when this has ever been our reality; egoless. How many times have you beaten yourself up for making an error, striking out, missing as shot, or losing a game?"

"All the time!"

"Yep, and you sure are hard on yourself. Just imagine learning to skip that part of hate and fear. Not feeling the need to yell at me, your mom, or anyone who crosses your path. Although it is a protection mechanism of the ego, it weakens you."

"Are you saying I should stop that?"

"Yep. It sounds like a crazy idea, doesn't it?"

"Damn right, it does!"

"I am just saying, if you can channel that energy to a place of strength, you will feel better about yourself and the people in the world. You won't feel as angry or be so upset. Maybe you will no longer find a need to scream at me."

"I know, and I am sorry. I tell you I am sorry whenever I'm upset."

"Yes, I know, and I'm thankful you are aware of it and that you apologize. I'm willing to bet, deep down, it makes you feel awful inside."

"Yeah, it does. But I don't know any other way. My coach yells and screams. Even the pros do it!" she exclaimed.

"Yeah, the common approach with coaches is to scream and yell at players. But that doesn't mean it's the right way to handle things."

"They toss clipboards." She smiled.

"Yeah, that too. Whenever your coach freaks out and screams, how does it make you feel? Does it motivate you to want to do better, or does he make you feel like crap and not want to play?"

"Definitely crap," she firmly replied.

"That approach might work for some people, like Kristy, your sister's softball trainer. She said she does better when she is yelled at. You, on the other hand, don't do well with that approach. And I don't either. Although I have learned to find motivation in it. At first, it sucks, because I think everyone is going to laugh at me or the coach is picking on me. Then I think through what happened and what the coach said, and I push myself to become better and no longer make the same mistake. Basically, too many coaches believe the only way to improve, motivate, and win is with fear and intimidation. And we end up believing that is the way to get better, by beating the shit out of ourselves and beating ourselves up. Don't you ever wonder why he is that way?"

"Well, yeah. All the time!"

"It is probably because he was brought up that way. And that doesn't make it right. The real champions and leaders learn from this and carve a different path. Plus, there's a difference when we are hard on ourselves from an energy of hate versus inner strength. Your coach coaches from fear and a little bit of anger, but also from love."

"Mostly anger," his daughter commented.

"He was probably brought up that way and may never know of any other way to coach. You just have to find that little bit of love in him. I see it. It took me a while, but I see it. He loves the sport, he loves coaching, and he loves the team. The way he expresses it is up for debate."

"But why does he treat his daughter like crap? He is so mean to her and makes her cry all the time."

"I see that too, sweetie. I wish I had an answer. I'm sure that was how he was raised, how his parents— and maybe his coaches—treated him. There are not many coaches who coach from a perspective of love. I do know of a couple, though: your grandfather and great-grandfather."

"Really?"

"Yep! Through the power of love. They were very successful coaches. Listen, I am not saying you shouldn't be angry. Anger often is an intensity of love in disguise. So, if you love yourself, love what you do, and feel an intensity, a strong desire to get better and win, that is far better than hatred and self-defeating self-talk. I do believe that we can win, even dominate, and be number one by embracing the energy of love."

"Yeah, right." She scoffed, rolling her eyes once again. "Sounds boring and lame. No one likes a happy, nice player."

"Is it really lame? And how do you know? Have you tried it?"

"Well, no," she answered and paused. "Now that I think about it, I have always been nice. But people can be such jerks, so I push them away by being mean."

"Well, aren't you a chip off the old block." Her dad smiled. "I was like that, in a bad way, for a long time."

"You still are, Dad."

"Thanks for the reminder. Yes, I am aware. I do my best to tell you when I'm acting like a jerk, and then explain why I acted that way. I don't excuse it, and I'm trying to understand it, so I will no longer do it. Because I know for a fact that hate and doubt do nothing other than create more hate and doubt. It becomes tiresome and depressing. All I am saying is pay attention to your self-talk. What do you say to yourself when you are nervous or make a mistake or an error? I bet you're not very nice to yourself. In fact, you are probably meaner to yourself than anyone else has ever been."

"Yeah, sure, Dad." She smiled, knowing he was right.

"Just imagine your belief system, or should I say your 'doubt system,' changing. Your self-talk would change as well. When you lose a point, a game, a set, or even a match at tennis or any sport, you say to yourself: 'It's OK. I love you. Next time, don't take your eye off the ball.' Imagine that! Winning with love. It can happen.

"One day, you just might realize that the only constant in life is love. Not hate. Not fear. Love. Love endures all. I am going to send you a copy of an article I recently read." Wayne grabbed his iPhone out of his back pocket. He held the screen to his face to unlock the phone. With his right thumb, he touched the bottom of the screen and swept his finger in an upward motion, as though he was flicking something off of the screen. He tapped the screen with his thumb, then he tapped it again and a few more times. "OK. I just sent the article to you," he said. His daughter's phone rang, signaling the incoming text message. "Please take the time to read it when you get a chance."

"OK. Thanks, Dad!"

"Yep. Love you!"

"Love you, too!"

"OK. Let's get out of here." They hopped into his car and turned on the music as loudly as they could, playing the song "Brilliant" by Shinedown, and drove off.

Learn from the Empty Boat Story[55]

"Anger doesn't just happen to us," says Buddhist teacher and author John Daido Loori. "If we're able to catch an angry thought as it's budding, we can let it go." The following Buddhist parable supports his insight.

With permission from the monastery abbot, a monk borrowed an old boat and rowed out into the middle of a lake for his afternoon meditation session. It was a truly peaceful place to meditate as the boat gently floated. After more than an hour of undisturbed silence, he felt the bump of another boat against his. Though his eyes were still closed, he could feel anger swelling within at the careless boatman who didn't prevent the lake collision.

Upon opening his eyes, all he saw was an empty boat, which he realized had become untied from the dock and merely drifted out into the lake, bumping up against his. Immediately, the monk experienced a flash of enlightenment, one that would serve him well for the rest of his life. "The anger is within me," he thought to himself. "All anger needs is a bump from the outside to be triggered and provoked out of me."

From that moment on, whenever another person irritated him and he could feel even the slightest anger rising, he gently reminded himself: "The other person is an empty, floating boat. The anger is within me."

Opposite George

"Lesson 153: In my defenselessness my safety lies. …The world provides no safety. It is rooted in attack, and all its "gifts" of seeming safety are illusory deceptions. It attacks, and then attacks again. No peace of mind is possible where danger threatens thus. The world gives rise but to defensiveness. For threat brings anger, anger makes attack seem reasonable, honestly provoked, and righteous in the name of self-defense. Yet is defensiveness a double threat? For it attests to weakness, and sets up a system of defense that cannot work. Now are the weak still further undermined, for there is treachery without and still a greater treachery within. The mind is now confused, and knows not where to turn to find escape from its imaginings."[56]
— *A Course in Miracles*

"The wise endowed with equanimity of intellect, abandon attachment to the fruits of actions, which bind one to the cycle of life and death. By working in such consciousness, they attain the state beyond all suffering."[57]
— *The Bhagavad Gita*

The War Within. Self-Realization.

It was another Friday evening. Wayne was on the phone, in yet another deep conversation with Gary DeAngelis. Pacing the floor of his daughter's bedroom, where he found seclusion while she was away at a friend's house for the weekend, Wayne spoke passionately and somewhat rapidly. He would sometimes skip taking a breath because he did not want to miss a beat or be interrupted.

"Have you ever read the Bhagavad Gita?" Wayne asked Gary.

"What's that?"

"It is an ancient Hindu scripture. It means, the 'song of God,' or the 'song of the Lord.'" Wayne said as he paced the room.

"Never heard of it."

"Well, it's pretty amazing and powerful. Some say it is the Hindu equivalent of the New Testament."

"Oh, really? Interesting."

"It is such a great work. It applies to everyone, regardless of faith or background. But it took me a long time to grasp it after many times of reading the book."

"That's like reading the Bible. No matter how many times you read it, you learn something new with each reading," Gary commented.

"Yes, I agree. After listening to the audiobook several times, I was able to apply it to everyday life. And, yes, each time I learned something new, or another part resonated with me."

"Oh. Like what?"

"Do you remember when I had that falling-out with my brother?"

"Oh yeah. I remember! He said some pretty malicious things."

"Yeah." Wayne sighed. "You don't have to remind me."

"Did he ever apologize?"

"Not really. Although we did speak. It certainly was not an apology, but more of a bullshit, meaningless conversation because our mother wanted things to be better between us. Although, he called with an empty and less than half-hearted attempt to reconnect, for our mother's sake. Not because he felt that he needed to apologize."

"Well, he said some pretty awful things, which cannot be taken back. Plus, he threatened you!"

"I know, but I'm trying to move on. And the Bhagavad Gita helped."

"How so?"

"Well, I read chapter one numerous times. The title of the chapter is 'The War Within.' Prince Arjuna is about to go into war against his family and friends, and he doesn't want to kill them. So, on the morning of the great battle, he turns to Sri Krishna, his friend and spiritual adviser, and asks him for guidance."

"Did he go into battle?"

"Yes, he did. It was a very intriguing dialogue between Arjuna and Krishna. Although Arjuna did not want to go into battle, Krishna said it was his duty in this life. In the end, Arjuna said he would do the will of Sri Krishna." Wayne paced the room as he spoke, stopping momentarily to take a sip from his water bottle. "Although, I'm not going into battle. Anyway, you should read it. Plus, the various interpretations of the Gita are very interesting. Sort of like the various versions and interpretations of the Bible."

"What do you mean?"

"Well, I think the big question about the Gita is whether or not it condones the acts of war and killing. So, if you read it, make sure you read chapter one a couple times. It is a powerful spiritual work, which is really about the human battle with the self. I was so upset by what my brother had said. It didn't help matters that we were in the middle of the pandemic farce. I was already pissed off because of that, which didn't help matters. My mother would not have made it home after being admitted to the hospital. They would have intubated her, and that would have been the last time we saw her. The entire thing was a hoax meant to control people and even kill them."

"Yeah, you told me." Gary sighed in disagreement.

"Listen, Gary. Like I said before, it's pretty fucking clear what's going on ..."

"Yes, I get it. You told me. Do we have to get into this again?"

"No. If you or anyone else hasn't seen through the bullshit, then most likely you never will. Sort of like the Sermon on the Mount. There were the mockers, the perplexed, and the believers. Not everyone believed Jesus's sermon. At the time, I was trying to process everything, the pandemic farce along with what my brother had said. Plus, I had to help my mother. There were plenty of armchair quarterbacks who would sweep in. And the moment they saw how frail she had become and how sick she was getting, they would panic. Their immediate reaction was to send her to the doctor, or even worse, the ER. Remember, this was in the thick of the farce, when people would enter the hospitals but never leave. After swooping in and creating more havoc, they would then leave, go back to living their lives, and leave things a messs to be cleaned up. All that was accomplished was more stress and anxiety for our mother.

"I was trying to process everything that was happening. After my bother attacked me, I needed to process my feelings. I wrestled with going to war. Did I need to protect myself, and possibly retaliate? If so, was it justified? This is where chapter one of the Bhagavad Gita was a tremendous help. I felt like Arjuna on the battlefield. Not wanting to go into battle and having to harm his brothers, cousins, friends, and family. Of course, in our world and society, there's no question about it, we must go to war and retaliate! This world condones war. Always has and always will, until and unless we change."

"Do you really believe that?"

"I don't know." Wayne paused and thought for a moment. "Well, on second thought, yes. Although, deep down, I don't believe it is the way to be. It just doesn't sit well with me. The thought always crosses my mind, though. And I know this is the ego wanting to fight. I don't want to buy into it, and I'd like to believe there is another way to exist. This is on the level of higher consciousness where war, attack, and hatred do not exist. It only exists in the human realm."

"That is a little too deep for me. All I know is your brother was an asshole and should not have done what he did." Gary paused.

"True, but I cannot be attacked if I don't allow it. Safety is the complete relinquishment of attack,[58]" Wayne quoted from *A Course in Miracles.* "So, when someone gets pissed off and attacks, they are attacking themselves. They are so angry at their perspective of the world and themselves that they attack. I don't have to accept it or receive it if I choose not to."

"But aren't you upset? Aren't you worried about him coming after you?"

"Only when I talk about it. Otherwise, I'm not concerned. If he attacks me, then so be it. It will only hurt him, not me. I'm tired of talking about it. But, if you get a chance to read the Gita, make sure you read chapter one, 'The War Within'; chapter two, 'Self-Realization'; and chapter sixteen, 'Two Paths.' If you'd like, I will be happy to give you a copy of the book."

"If you don't mind. That would be great."

Opposite George

"Death means the attainment of heaven; victory means the enjoyment of the earth. Therefore rise up, Arjuna, resolved to fight!"
—*The Bhagavad Gita,* 2:37[59]

"If you fight, you will either be slain on the battlefield and go to the celestial abodes, or you will gain victory and enjoy the kingdom on earth. Therefore, arise with determination, O son of Kunti, and be prepared to fight." As Arjuna's spiritual teacher, Sri Krishna's task now is to rouse Arjuna from his despair and set him on the way to Self-realization.
—*The Bhagavad Gita*[60]

The Buddha Laughed, and Jesus Wept

Wayne's conversation with Gary continued late into the night. The conversation went even deeper as they fed off each other's energy. Gary viewed the world through rose-colored glasses and drank from a half-full glass, while Wayne drank from a half-empty glass and saw the world through cloudy glasses. But he realized the sun was always shining behind the clouds. And, in order for the glass to be half-empty, he was beginning to realize the glass must, also, be half full.

"So, apparently, Jesus Christ's life was unaccounted for from around the age of twelve until age thirty."

"Yep, no one knows his whereabouts," Gary replied in a matter-of-fact tone.

"I find that very interesting."

"Of course you do," Gary answered somewhat sarcastically with a slight chuckle.

"Well, Gary." Wayne paused. "Where was he? What was he doing? Who was he hanging around over the course of eighteen years?"

Gary chuckled, "No one knows."

"How convenient, that no one knows his whereabouts for nearly twenty years. And people are perfectly comfortable looking the other way and brushing it under the carpet. Then he shows up, preaching the gospel and performing miracles. Where the heck was he?"

"Maybe he was running around causing trouble?" Gary commented.

Wayne was speechless. He never thought he would hear those words from Gary, a devout Catholic. But he was always a reasonable guy. He would speak the truth when it needed to be heard, and he was also open to learning new things or hearing a different take on the world.

Wayne asked, "What if Jesus strayed off his path? Maybe he experienced moments of heightened emotion, possibly frustration, or dare I say anger?"

Gary chuckled again. "That's the missing part of Jesus's life. No one knows." He repeated himself.

"What is truly inspiring about Jesus is not what is captured in the Bible and scripture, but the years of his life that are unaccounted for."

"Why's that?" Gary asked.

"Having no account of his whereabouts, followers of Christ are fairly adamant that Christ was somewhere on his path. They have no proof one way or another, but they will not stray from what they hope he was doing."

"I am not in disagreement there."

"So what if the Messiah strayed off course? When it comes to the story of Jesus Christ, there is so much invested in who he was, being the Messiah, his crucifixion and his resurrection." Wayne took a breath followed by a drink from his water bottle. "I read something explaining away his unaccounted years. No proof or verification. It was explained away because they said it did not sound like him. Hold on a second."

Wayne opened the browser on his iPhone and typed in the search bar, "Jesus's childhood the missing years." He pressed *Go*, clicked on the first link, and began to read. "'However, these 'gospels' present a child who is sullen and uses miracles for entertainment rather than doing the will of God. Neither of these attributes fits with the character of Christ.'"[61] Wayne paused and took a breath. "Isn't it convenient to simply explain away his missing years by saying that it didn't sound like him to act like a teenager?"

Gary shook his head and smiled. "I get it, Wayne. No one knows. And, yes, the church is not going to hint at or say he acted like a normal human being."

"Well, good. Then we can all agree that we really don't know Jesus's character or whereabouts during his teens and twenties."

"No argument here."

"It's a little convenient to blindly assume he was on his path and never strayed. It would make for an even greater story of the Messiah. Not only was he the chosen one who performed miracles, but he strayed off his path for a while to find his way back. With all of the talk and great stories about second chances, how fucking amazing would that be? Wouldn't it make for an even better story if he were led astray and corrected course? Wouldn't that give the rest of humanity hope that they, too, can correct course and be saved?"

"Sure, I guess so. But it's not that simple. No one is going to admit that's where he was and what he was doing," Gary stated.

"Of course not, because that would mean there's a flaw, or error, in the story of Jesus. His mother was a virgin, yet miraculously, she gave birth to Jesus. His father was not his paternal father and wasn't really sure how Mary became pregnant. So, for argument's sake, let's just say Jesus grew up in an angry and confused household. It's possible." Wayne continued, "Maybe Jesus was running around looking for trouble and loved chasing women. Once in a while, after a bottle or two of wine, he would let loose, finding himself in a fight and enraged by life. Sounds far-fetched, right? But the story of his mother —being a virgin, getting pregnant, and no one really knowing who the father was—creates a bit of tension in an egoic world. Not such a far-fetched story, huh?

Wayne continued, "Maybe he went away. Could it be possible that he was lost and confused? Did he face his anger and fears, which were catalysts for his awakening as the Messiah? Because sometimes, in order to awaken to our power and truth, we must suffer and experience hell before we can achieve enlightenment and experience higher consciousness."

"Interesting take on his missing years," Gary interjected. "I'm not so sure that's what happened, though."

"Of course not, Gary!" Wayne retorted. "You have been brought up your entire life believing in one story. I mean, could it be that he went away to spend those years alone in isolation, meditating and praying which led to his enlightenment? Quite possible," Wayne emphatically commented. "For most people who achieve enlightenment, they have to 'go away' and spend time alone, in meditation or prayer, so they can align with and channel the divine spirit. And, when he returned in his thirties, he began spreading his gospel, performing miracles, healing, and so on. What a powerful and inspiring story!" Wayne paused to take a sip from his water bottle.

"And even more devastating and heartbreaking is the inconvenient truth that Jesus was crucified by the very brothers and sisters he was healing. And over two thousand years later, we haven't changed much."

"You know, ever since you mentioned the Buddha and how he experienced suffering, I've spent a lot of time thinking about that. And it has opened my eyes to a deeper understanding of Christ."

"Really?" Wayne was again caught off guard by Gary's comment. "Wow! I didn't know that. That's wonderful. Thank you, Gary!" Wayne was so happy to hear that Gary was in fact listening. "You know, although I may sound angry, I'm really not. When I speak, it is with an intensity of love. I love the story of Jesus, and I love the Buddha. And they taught and believed the same thing."

"That's it! That was the statement that got my attention," Gary said.

"So what if Jesus didn't die for our sins, but rather, he died because of our sins?"

"You know, the first time I heard you say that," Gary paused, "I was pissed off. But the more I listen and think about it, the more it makes sense."

"I am so happy to hear that. Maybe it's about time everyone sets aside their egoic tendencies for him. He gave up his life, apparently for us, yet we will not even consider giving up our egoic tendencies for him. And Jesus Christ's second coming will be realized the moment we awaken to the Kingdom of God within ourselves. He said, 'The Kingdom of God is within you.' He was saying we have His power. The Kingdom of God is in each and every one of us, if we awaken to His power, which is within each and every one of us! And then there's the Buddha."

"What about the Buddha?"

"The Buddha's birth name was Siddhartha Gautama. He was a prince, born into a lavish life. He had everything one could wish for: food, clothes, wine, women, and wealth. His life was one of luxury. Eventually, he fathered a son, whom he named Fetter, which is translated as 'ball and chain.'"

"Really? Ball and chain?"

"Yep. Apparently, he named his son 'ball and chain.' Siddhartha Gautama was enchanted with the outside world and wanted to experience it, so he snuck out of the kingdom. On his adventure outside the walls of the kingdom, he encountered a sick person, an old person, and then a corpse. He had never experienced a world like this before. It frightened and intrigued him, so he decided to abandon his wife, son, and princely life to pursue enlightenment."

Gary interrupted, "He left his wife and son?"

"Yep. He had human tendencies, which makes his story even more powerful and intriguing. Long story short, his realization upon attaining enlightenment and becoming the Buddha was that suffering is a natural part of the human experience. In that realization, he recognized suffering for what it is: a teacher."

"I was always led to believe that the Buddha was about avoiding suffering."

"You know, that's not the first time I've heard someone say that. He saw suffering and realized we could not avoid it because it is a natural part of being human. What he taught was that suffering was going to happen regardless, and it was up to us to decide if we wanted to experience pain and sorrow from it or use it as a teacher and a guide. Sort of like losing the big game. We always learn lessons from a loss, but we don't allow it to devastate us, and we don't give up. We learn from it because it's a natural part of competition."

"Wow! So true. It can be applied to work, as well."

"Yep. And you already do that, Gary. I believe you are on the doorstep of Buddhahood; you've just never realized it." Wayne smiled. "The Buddha sought enlightenment. Jesus sought enlightenment. Sri Krishna helped Arjuna seek understanding. When Jesus returned from many years away, he was enlightened. He healed. He fed hundreds. He turned water into wine. He was the Son of God. And then he was crucified. Jesus had the ability to perform miracles, to heal and even raise the dead, but he couldn't prevent his very own crucifixion. How? Why?"

"Because he died for our sins."

"Stop reciting what you have been told to say. Why would he do that? Who does that? What does that do for anyone? How about Jesus died because of our sins, and we were not capable of being saved? He didn't even save himself. He was the Messiah. He had the power to perform miracles, and he could not perform a miracle and save himself? Come on!

"And there's The Buddha who accepted suffering as a part of human existence. And he did not take it on as his burden to carry. Prince Arjuna reiterates to Sri Krishna that he is unable to cope with his current situation, i.e., suffering, and requests Sri Krishna to be his spiritual teacher and guide him on the proper path of action."

Wayne continued, "Jesus was also aware that suffering was a part of human existence. Each of them experienced the same thing. Each of them wanted to achieve enlightenment and share their teachings with others to help them on their personal journeys. Jesus Christ took on the suffering of the world, and apparently, he did it for us. So why hasn't anyone ever considered that he died because of our sins, rather than for our sins? That creates an entirely different picture, doesn't it?"

"Yes, it does."

"We all suffer. That's the human experience, and apparently, there is no other way to exist. The cause of our suffering is the ego. The mind. Although I believe there is another way. Which is what Jesus, the Buddha, and Sri Krishna taught. It is higher consciousness, or pure positive energy, which doesn't have an opposite. There is nothing but light. No fear, no jealousy, no hatred, no fear; and the egoic mind does not exist.

"The human experience is a devolution from divinity. Despite the miracles and abundance surrounding us on earth we are often blind to, and ignorant of, it. And Jesus Christ is in each and every one of us. He healed. Pay attention to the miracles of the human body. The human body heals. Yet we dismiss our own healing power.

"It is a dangerous, slippery slope to be so blindly faithful and dedicated to one religion and faith, in that you disregard other faiths. Putting all of our spiritual eggs in one basket and one story, hoping that he will magically return one day to save us, is a little shortsighted. And apparently, only those who are believers can be saved, while the rest of the world, the nonbelievers, are doomed. A loving God would never place such a demand on the world." Wayne took another sip from his water bottle and continued speaking while Gary listened. "With man this is impossible, but with God all things are possible."

"Matthew, 19:26." Gary stated the Bible verse.

"That verse from the Bible applies to all human beings who align with higher awareness and God consciousness. And what happens when Jesus does not come back and save us? What then?"

"We're a bunch of fools," Gary muttered.

"Just a bunch of fools!" Wayne repeated. "We are giving our power away. And this isn't what Jesus wanted. Waiting for one person to magically reappear one day to save us is ludicrous. Even if this were true and he returned, we wouldn't even recognize him. We are so blind and ignorant that we would doubt his words and we would crucify him all over again. Please pay attention. Jesus was trying to show us that the second coming is our awakening. This is the moment when we remove all of our egoic intentions and awaken to the Kingdom of God within ourselves! We have the power to do as Jesus did! But when the world is filled with fear, fueled by the ego, our awakening will not manifest.

"The good news is that our awakening is possible and has always been possible. It is up to each of us because it is within each and every one of us. Believing the lies of the ego, we have already doomed ourselves to hell. We create our own destinies of fear and suffering, over and over. The moment we awaken and rise up to realize the miracle Jesus was trying to show his brothers and sisters, we will be saved. This is higher consciousness."

"Amen, brother," Gary said on the other end of the phone.

"Oh yeah, a few more great things about Jesus to ponder: What were his accolades? What made him the Messiah? Did he go to university to study asceticism, healing, and how to become a messiah? Jesus Christ was a carpenter. This blue-collar worker, who was the Messiah, is celebrated and praised thousands of years later. Today, in our highly evolved world, in order to be worthy and fit in with society, you must have a degree, letters after your name, and lots of money. That's a facade. Jesus was a carpenter! And guess what? Our society pooh-poohs blue-collar workers!

"I was speaking with a successful local businessman who happened to be an electrician. He was telling me that his youngest son asked him if he was speaking at career day at his son's high school. Sadly, he said, he wasn't."

"Really? Why?"

"Are you ready for this? The West Chester School District did not invite him to speak because they did not consider blue-collar work a career."

"Bullshit! You're lying."

"I wish I was, but this is a true story. These fucking idiots do not acknowledge blue-collar work as a legitimate career, hence he could not speak at career day. Who built the goddamn school? Who the hell set up the electrical system at the school? Builders, construction workers, plumbers, and electricians! That's our local school system for you. Idiots!"

"I am blown away. Please tell me you're joking."

"Nope. This is for real!"

"Oh man." Gary sighed.

"So Jesus did not need academics in order to attain enlightenment, because he was aligned with the energy of higher consciousness. The Buddha was a prince, the son of a wealthy king, and renounced all of it. These spiritual icons, leaders, and heroes had no advanced educations or degrees. A diploma is not needed for that. The more we learn and the more educated we become, it seems the more paralyzed, single-minded, and ignorant we are. Our ego tells us how great we are, that we are better than others. The Buddha didn't do this, Jesus didn't do this, and neither did Sri Krishna or Arjuna. Are you still there, Gary?" Wayne asked.

"Yeah. Sorry, I was intently listening. Keep going. I love this!"

"OK, thanks." Wayne continued, "Our reality, our existence, is fashioned after Jesus Christ and his crucifixion. We believe in fear. We believe in tragedy. We want to believe in a happy ending, but we are always looking over our shoulders for a devastating and tragic end, just like the story of the Messiah! Just imagine if the Buddha was the Messiah instead.

"There was little drama in the Buddha's life. Sure, he was a young prince with wealth, women, and all the things anyone would wish for, and yet he wanted to explore the world. Sure, he did some things that others might not agree with, like naming his son Fetter, and leaving his son and wife behind.

"Think about Jesus and his unaccounted years. Maybe he, too, had a wife and a son whom he left behind to seek enlightenment. Does that make him less of a man or no longer the Messiah?

"Like I said before, that's a good portrayal of life's journey. We may make mistakes, but the church likes the drama of it all and labels them sins. They are errors, and when we align with higher awareness, we can reconnect with Source, achieve enlightenment and God consciousness.

"Maybe the tipping point for Jesus was the moment his eyes were opened to a world of suffering, which triggered a strong desire to understand and seek enlightenment. And when he did, he taught others what he'd learned. Just as the Buddha did.

"Jesus's path was very similar to the Buddha's. The only difference was the Buddha was not an outcast and was not beaten, whipped, stoned, tortured, and ultimately crucified. The Buddha did not take on the suffering of his brothers and sisters and the world, as Jesus did. The Buddha's story is boring in comparison to the story of Jesus Christ. And the rest of the Buddha's life was relatively uneventful.

"He lived to a ripe old age, teaching the Four Noble Truths and the Eightfold Path. When he felt it was time to leave the human realm, he left. No drama. No murder. No tragedy. He just left. Although, it has been said he consumed bad food, maybe poisoned food, which led to his death. Either way, he knew it was his time.

"Can you imagine what our reality would be like if the Buddha was the Messiah? Hollywood would be so boring. We would live peaceful and happy lives without tragedy. We would not be paralyzed by fear and doubt. We would not look over our shoulders for tragedy to strike. In fact, we would see suffering for what it is: a teacher and a guide. What a wonderful existence!

"But we have been conditioned to believe in hatred, war, death, and devastation. So, once again, the second coming of Christ is in our hands. He is not going to show up at your front door to save you. Christ consciousness is within you and me. It has always been, but we have tuned it out and are no longer aware that it is within each and every one of us. The only way we will achieve higher consciousness is by leaving our egoic tendencies at the altar and by going toward love." Wayne rested.

"I am blown away by all of this, Wayne! Thank you for sharing this with me. I've never heard it said in this way. I still am hesitant, but I see what you are getting at."

"Another thing about the Buddha's awakening: it was partly due to the realization that his suffering, through extreme asceticism, very well could have led to his death. He'd surrendered himself completely for many years, and it hadn't worked. On the verge of death, he remembered something. He realized that if he achieved enlightenment, he would be too weak to enjoy it, share it, and teach it to others.

"He understood that his body required nourishment in order to live. He needed to regain his strength in order to share his awakening with his fellow ascetics. His realization was that there would be no point in enlightenment if he died as a result.

"And then he ate! He accepted a bowl of rice from the ordinary, kind heart of a girl. It was from grace. And he remembered something: that he could not do it completely on his own. It was from the divine. He remembered his wife and his son. When he took the food, he saw that life is painful, and life involves change, and this was still a problem. Next, his ascetics turned away in disgust. He would then look within and trust himself. He became the Buddha."

It was late and Gary had to get some rest, "Dude, I am sorry, but I have to hit the hay. I'm tired, especially after hearing that."

"OK. I should get some shut eye, as well. Thank you for listening."

"Anytime Wayne. You know I enjoy our conversations, no matter where they take us. Have a good night."

"You, too."

"Peace!"

Opposite George

"Crucifixion wasn't really the hard thing for Jesus; the hard thing was incarnation. Crucifixion and what followed from it—his death and resurrection—were simply the pathway along which infinite consciousness could return to its natural state. What was really hard for infinite consciousness was to come into the finite world in the first place. With nothing to gain from the human adventure—nothing to prove, nothing to achieve, and a dangerously unboundaried heart that left him defenseless against the hard edges of this world—Jesus came anyway: that claims Bernadette Roberts, was the real crucifixion!"[62]
—*The Wisdom Jesus*

Source

It was late morning. Wayne and Sue were enjoying a cup of coffee and conversation as they typically did when they had a break from things. "Humans have one thing in common." Wayne sipped his water. "It's a spark for being alive. We will do the darndest things to stay alive, even if these things cause harm and even bring on death. It is a contradictory approach to life, and it's quite insane."

"Survival of the fittest," she commented.

"Well, I wouldn't necessarily call it that. Because, if that were the case, why are there so many idiots and unfit people still surviving?"

"That's a good point. So then, what are you talking about?"

"There is this spark that seems to guide us along the path of life. Some people seem to survive, living long lives despite being ignorant of the world around them. They seem oblivious to their surroundings, even putting themselves in danger, but somehow, harm does not come to them."

"Like your friend Nate."

"Yes. He's a perfect example. A really nice guy, but just seems oblivious to everything. He does the most idiotic things, and somehow, some way, he comes out unscathed."

"True. Although he has had his fair share of missteps."

"Yeah, I guess you're right. People like him may have a setback in the form of an accident, injury, or bad luck, but this 'force' somehow keeps them safe and alive." Wayne raised his hands in the air, gesturing air quotes, emphasizing force. "While driving their cars they seem oblivious to the traffic around them, missing their turns, taking the wrong turns, cutting people off, not seeing oncoming traffic; and yet they arrive safely at their destinations. And these setbacks don't deter them, either."

"I do that a lot. I miss my turns, but I always get back on track."

"Yes, you do." Wayne laughed. "That always amazes me, because I notice everything around me. I even notice you while I'm on my way out, driving down the street from our home, and you drive past me in the opposite direction while returning home. But you never see me. Yet, I see you every time."

"Yeah, I don't know. I always have my eyes straight ahead on the road, I guess." She smirked and shrugged her shoulders.

"And there are others who are very aware of their surroundings and can see potential dangers ahead of them and avoid them. At the end of the day, both arrive at their destinations safely. Not always, but generally, everyone does. So, I wonder, what is it that keeps us here? What is this power or force that keeps us here and keeps us safe?"

"Maybe it's the desire everyone has that makes us fight to stay alive?"

"Oh yeah. That's a good one. On top of that, what is this mysterious power that heals us? Is it the Holy Spirit? Or maybe Chi, prana, the Tao, or Brahma?"

"Maybe it's the force. 'May the force be with you.'" She smiled as she quoted the movie, *Star Wars*.

"If I were to choose one word, I think it is love that keeps us safe. Love is what wills us to nurture and care for one another rather than destroy and hurt." Wayne grabbed his water bottle, unscrewed the top, and took a sip. "And I'm not talking about the love we all chase and fall for. Not the love portrayed on television and in the movies. I'm talking about a sort of love that is a higher awareness."

"Are you talking about God?" she asked.

"Yes. I just didn't want to say it because there are so many different connotations when mentioning God. The two most common responses are to either tune out and turn away, or to call me a blasphemer and tell me to never utter the Lord's name in vain. I am seeking understanding. So maybe this power is a love that knows only goodness, healing, and peace. Because the ego creates division and separation. The ego creates so many different approaches to God, which creates more division and separation. At the end of the day, most religions, faiths, and belief systems worship the same power, the same God. This God energy is associated with what quite possibly gives us life: Source. It is the energy that allows us to think, smell, see, hear, taste, and touch."

"I once read that there is something like four thousand to ten thousand religions in the world, and over forty thousand different Christian denominations," she added.

"I'm not surprised. It supports what I've believed all along."

"What's that?"

"It wasn't that I didn't believe in God or a higher awareness. It was that I did not believe in one version versus another. It just didn't make sense to me that one believer in Christ would say their version of the Bible was better than someone else's. That's just stupid." Wayne paused to gather his thoughts. "I should clarify that. It's stupid that people would end up fighting and hating one another over their versions of the Bible. I am OK with different versions of Christ's story, but I'm not OK with fighting over whose version is best. We are all praying to and believing in the same God."

"What if there's more than one God?"

"Well, that would make things interesting. I'm OK with that. God comes in many different shapes and sizes. This is the human being trying to make sense of and understand life. But we will remain lost if we believe our God is better than someone else's God, or if we say there can only be one God. Although, from the human dualistic experience, the one-God approach makes sense. It is easier to believe in one God and a devil, or demon, Mara." Wayne read a quote from *A Course in Miracles*. "'Spirit has no levels, and all conflict arises from the concept of levels.'[66]

"Plus, many people mindlessly worship without truly connecting with God, Yahweh, Brahma, Allah, Krishna, and so on. I learned from Gary how to pray when he said that most people pray 'to God' instead of praying 'with God.' It's that simple. Connecting with God, Yahweh, Brahma, Allah, Krishna, Source, or the Supreme is about releasing all egoic attachment and allowing God energy to flow to and through you. Most people get stuck in their respective belief system and have a difficult time opening themselves up to infinite possibilities. Even if someone has no belief, no religion, or no god, they are still alive and they have life. So, we must ask ourselves, what is it that gives us life? What is it that keeps us safe and alive? How can this not pique people's curiosity?"

"Yep," she commented. "But I also think people don't think much about it because it's inconceivable and scares the shit out of them to go down that rabbit hole because there is no way out."

"Chi, prana, and Holy Spirit can be called Source, or the Supreme. It is the energy that beats our hearts and gives us life. Doesn't it make people curious to know what this 'life energy' is and where it comes from? Because no one seems to know.

"Before I forget … Back to the different versions of Christianity. I must reiterate this point, the inane teachings of the church about those who do not follow Christ and renounce their sins will all be doomed to hell, is ignorant. What about those who believe in the Buddha or Lord Krishna? The church says they are all doomed to hell because they haven't accepted Christ. This is nowhere in the vicinity of Christ consciousness or God consciousness. Christ did not teach 'my way or the highway.' He taught 'come with me.' God is not a vengeful God. This is of the ego."

"No argument here. Despite spending my life growing up in the church, with my mother deeply involved in the church, I questioned it as well. I just never understood the fear. The pandemic confirmed for me that most people of faith are just repeating words and are not aligned with the true teachings of Christ."

"I agree. I am not by any means disparaging God, but rather, I seek to understand and connect with God or higher awareness. Usually, when people fear for their lives or experience something life-threatening or something extremely pleasurable, they say, 'God! Oh my God! God, please save me.'"

Sue shifted the topic slightly. "It is quite entertaining and a little ludicrous that, whenever people scream to or praise God, they look up toward the sky. God is not a bearded man, hovering in the clouds above, wearing a flowing white gown or a toga."

"I agree. I believe God is all around us. God is within us, and we are of God." Wayne interjected. "Is Jesus really going to show up at our doorstep one day and save us?" Wayne repeated to Sue what he'd previously shared with Gary. "Imagine this! The power is within us to awaken to higher consciousness. What if this is the second coming of Christ? We all have the power Jesus had. He did say, 'The Kingdom of God is within you.' Jesus suffered because this is the human experience. The Buddha suffered, as well. How they handled it was drastically different!"

Wayne continued, "There is a God. There is no god. The choice is yours. We have free will. We don't have free will. You get to choose. I loved God. I hated God. I screamed at the top of my lungs toward the heavens above, 'Fuck you! There is no God!' I tried my best to believe in God. And I gave it my best effort to deny God. All the while, the decision has been mine to make.

"God is good. It feels good. My decisions carry weight, and my body tells me about my decisions. Of all of the times I chose hatred, of all the times I have renounced God—which felt fantastic in the moment—the energy and words conveyed did not sit well with me. No matter how many times I tried to deny God, I kept coming back, yearning for an answer. It seemed as though it was a matter of choice; hatred and anger or Love and God. And hatred seemed so much easier. If I could push others away, keeping them at a distance, that meant I would remain safe from any attack. But pushing them away did not sit well with me. Although, pushing them away did serve a purpose for a time. It allowed me to see clearly without interference from the opinions of others."

"Sure, but pushing people away versus going away is different," Sue interjected.

"True. You're right about that; and for that, I am sorry."

"About what?"

"Pushing people away. Even pushing you away at times."

"It's OK. I'm sure I have my quirks." Sue smiled.

"I finally did figure out that there is a difference between pushing someone away and going away to reflect. Keeping a distance to reflect and reset is perfectly fine. Most people who are enlightened have to go away or find solitude in order to reconnect with higher consciousness. "It has become abundantly clear to me that we have a choice."

"You think too much," Sue smiled. "Doesn't it make you tired?"

"To be honest, yes. But I can't help it."

"What about what you often say about 'Being Here Now?" Sue asked.

"I know," Wayne sighed. "I'm still working on it. Thank you for the reminder though."

Wayne and Sue enjoyed their conversation and coffee a little while longer before they had to get on with the day and take their kids to their activities.

Opposite George

"When you have learned how to decide with God, all decisions become as easy and as right as breathing. There is no effort, and you will be led as gently as if you were being carried down a quiet path in summer."[63]
— *A Course in Miracles*

"Say, then, to your brother: I give you to the Holy Spirit as part of myself. I know that you will be released, unless I want to use you to imprison myself. In the name of my freedom I choose your release, because I recognize that we will be released together."[64]
— *A Course in Miracles*

"No prophecy ever came by the impulse of man, but men moved by the Holy Spirit spoke from God."[65]
— *2 Peter 1:21*

Spirit

"Spirit has no levels, and all conflict arises from the concept of levels."[66]
—*A Course in Miracles*

"Love created me like itself. I am in the likeness of my Creator. I cannot suffer, I cannot experience loss and I cannot die. I am not a body."[67]
—*A Course in Miracles*

Christian Trinity: Father, Son, and Holy Spirit

"Only one God, the Godhead consists of three distinct persons—the Father, Son, and Holy Spirit."[68]

God the Father

"God the Father—Jesus Christ referred to His Father as God."[69]

"Jesus said to her, "Do not cling to me, for I have not yet ascended to the Father; but go to my brothers and say to them, 'I am ascending to my Father and your Father, to my God and your God.'""[70]

—John 20:17

"God the Father created the universe and everything in it...God the Father is the Supreme Being, Creator, and Sustainer..."[72]

"In the beginning was the Word, and the Word was with God, and the Word was God."[73]

—John 1:1

God the Holy Spirit

"After declaring that God raised Christ from the dead, the New Testament goes on to credit the Holy Spirit with the resurrection."[74]

"Let it be known to all of you and to all the people of Israel that by the name of Jesus Christ of Nazareth, whom you crucified, whom God raised from the dead—by him this man is standing before you well."[75]

—Acts 4:10

"If the Spirit of him who raised Jesus from the dead dwells in you, he who raised Christ Jesus[a] from the dead will also give life to your mortal bodies through his Spirit who dwells in you."[76]

— Romans 8:11

Holy Spirit

"In which healing, prophecy, the expelling of demons (exorcism), and speaking in tongues (glossolalia) are particularly associated with the activity of the Spirit."[77]

"A perfectly holy and spotless God, free of any sin or darkness. He shares the strengths of God the Father and Jesus, such as omniscience, omnipotence, and eternality. Likewise, he is all-loving, forgiving, merciful and just."[78]

Chi

"Vital energy that is held to animate the body internally."[79]

Prana

A life breath.[80]

Hindu Trinity

Hindu Trinity, or Trimurti: Brahma—the creator, Vishnu—the sustainer, and Shiva—the destroyer.[81]

Brahma

The creator god of the Hindu sacred triad.[82, 83]

Vishnu

Vishnu is the Preserver and guardian of men, he protects the order of things (dharma) and he appears on earth in various incarnations (avatars) to fight demons and to maintain cosmic harmony.[84]

Shiva

May represent goodness, benevolence and serve as the Protector. He is also associated with Time, and particularly as the destroyer and creator of all things.[85]

Try to Realize the Truth—Choose Wisely.

Lying in bed, Wayne slowly opened his eyes and rolled over onto his back. Closing his eyes again, he counted to himself. *Three, two, one.* Taking a deep breath, he began counting down. *Ten, nine, eight, seven, six, five, four, three, two, one.* Somewhere after eight, he was free. Free of his body. As close as he could ever get to pure positive energy. No body. No resistance. Just the feelings of peace and ease. He was in flow.

Every morning, for a few seconds, he was free. Free from his body. Free from the worries of the world. Free from thought. Free from everything and connected only to Source. He always hoped he could remain a little longer, maybe forever, but he always returned.

Still lying in bed, he rubbed his eyes and stared at the ceiling. Laying in silence, the faithful ringing in his ears greeted him. Taking a deep breath, he recited his morning affirmations. "Spirit am I, a holy Son of God, free of all limits, safe and healed and whole, free to forgive, and free to save the world."[86] Wayne paused. Taking a breath, he began again. "I am not a body. I am free. For I am still as God created me."[87]

He repeated his affirmations a couple more times. "I am God's Son, complete and healed and whole, shining in the reflection of His love.[88] I am one with the very power that created me, and this power has given me the power to create my own circumstances. I rejoice in the knowledge that I can use my mind in any way I choose. I choose love, health, happiness, and prosperity."

He sat up, shifting his legs over the edge of the bed. His feet landed firmly on the ground. Resting his elbows upon his knees, he leaned forward and placed his forehead in the palms of his hands. He rubbed his eyes with the palms of his hands for a morning mini face massage. His hands came together, slowly sliding away from his face in a prayer pose. His chin rested upon the V shape formed with his thumbs and forefingers while his nose was propped upon the tips of his forefingers and middle fingers. With his eyes closed, Wayne thought about the nursery rhyme, "Row, Row, Row Your Boat."

Row, row, row your body,

Gently through your life.

Happily, happily, happily, happily,

Life is just a dream.

He managed to muster the energy to get up and start the day. He slowly rose to his feet and walked to the bathroom to brush his teeth. Wayne finished up and with a slight grumble, he moaned, "Ugh. Oh my God. I am so tired."

He walked out of the bedroom and headed toward the kitchen to get a cup of coffee. Upon entering the kitchen, he saw his wife, Sue. "Hey sweetie, I warmed up your coffee."

"Uh, OK." Wayne replied, a little surprised. *Warmed up my coffee? I haven't even had my first cup yet.* He wondered to himself. "Uh, great. Thanks," he mumbled.

Sue slid the cup of coffee across the kitchen table toward Wayne. "You know, I was thinking about what you said before."

"Huh?" Wayne mumbled silently, still a little confused since he just got out of bed. "Oh yeah, what was that?" He replied acting as though he knew what was going on.

"About choice. When I was going through my treatments I knew right then and there that I had to make a choice, because one wasn't going to be made for me. All I can say is, pay attention and choose wisely. I made my choice long ago." Sue firmly stated.

Although Wayne was still slightly confused, thinking he had just awoken from a night's sleep, he was aligned with what Sue was saying. Without skipping a beat, he replied, "I agree. We have a choice to believe in healing, Love, God, Chi, prana, Yahweh, or the Supreme, accepting and aligning with higher consciousness, or God consciousness or not. We can choose to not align with higher awareness and consciousness, and instead, believe in something else. The choice is ours. You have certainly proven that beyond a doubt.

"You made your decision to heal physically and miraculously you did exactly that!" Wayne smiled as a tear slid down his cheek. "I too have made my choice, to heal spiritually. Although, my journey continues. But I am no longer seeking, for I have found. Although, these egoic tendencies still tap me on the shoulder once in a while, wanting me to hate, retaliate, and fight. The ego is so afraid of no longer being relevant, that it will make us believe we cannot exist without it. When someone is aligned with Love and higher awareness—whether it is God consciousness, Christ consciousness, Buddha consciousness, Maya, samadhi, or Nirvana—it scares the shit out of the ego. So, I will lay them down to rest."

"Lay what down to rest?" Sue asked.

"My egoic tendencies." Wayne paused and then recited the following words, "Nothing real can be threatened. Nothing unreal exists. Herein lies the peace of God."[89]

Opposite George

"Do not try and bend the spoon. That's impossible.
Instead, only try to realize the Truth."
"What truth?"
"There is no spoon."
"There is no spoon?"
"Then you will see that it is not the spoon
the bends. It is only yourself."41
—*The Matrix, movie*

There is no spoon.
There is no beginning.
There is no end.
There is no birth.
There is no death.
I am a body.
I am not a body.
There is a God.
There is no God.
I have free will.
I don't have free will.
I have a choice.
You have a choice.
The choice is ours to make, but the ego will tell you otherwise.
So, choose wisely.

Definitions for Clarity and Contemplation

These 'definitions' are for your musing and contemplation. A word to one has an entirely different meaning to another.

Ego: Error, sin, fear. The ego is a wrong-minded attempt to perceive yourself as you wish to be, rather than as you are.[90]

Sin: Error.

God: Brahma, Allah, Krishna, Yahweh.

Source: Spirit, Holy Spirit, Chi, prana, Tao, Love, Supreme.

Bliss: Samadhi, Nirvana, Heaven.

Love: Bliss, Source; all that sustains life and is not fear, sin, ego, sickness, and separation.

The course does not aim at teaching the meaning of love, for that is beyond what can be taught. It does aim, however, at removing the blocks to the awareness of love's presence, which is your natural inheritance. The opposite of love is fear, but what is all-encompassing can have no opposite.[91]
— *A Course in Miracles*

Suggested Reading

I Am That, Nisargadatta Maharaj, 1973

The Perennial Philosophy, Aldous Huxley, 1945

Power vs. Force, David R. Hawkins, 2014

A Course in Miracles, Foundation for Inner Peace, 1975

The Bhagavad Gita

The Upanishads

The Mahabharata

The Bible

The Four Noble Truths

The Eightfold Path

Any book by Dr. Wayne Dyer

You Can Heal Your Life, Louise Hay, 1984

A Return to Love, Marianne Williamson, 1996

Tears to Triumph, Marianne Williamson, 2017

The Power of Now, Eckhart Tolle, 2004

A New Earth, Eckhart Tolle, 2008

Dying to Be Me, Anita Moorjani, 2012

Be Here Now, Ram Dass, 1971

The Wisdom Jesus, Cynthia Bourgeault, 2008

The pH Miracle, Shelley Redford Young, Robert O. Young PhD (Author), 2010

A Finger on the Magic of Life, Robert O. Young, 2016

"On the Origins of Cancer Cells," Otto Warburg, 1956

The Blood and Its Third Element, Dr. Antoine Bechamp, 2016

The Hidden Messages in Water, Masaru Emoto, 2005

Notes

Book

Foundation for Inner Peace, *A Course in Miracles* (Mill Valley, CA: Foundation for Inner Peace, 2007).

1. Foundation for Inner Peace, *A Course in Miracles* (Mill Valley, CA: Foundation for Inner Peace, 2007), ACIM, W-97.7:2

2. Foundation for Inner Peace, *A Course in Miracles* (Mill Valley, CA: Foundation for Inner Peace, 2007), ACIM, W-201.1:4-6

3. Foundation for Inner Peace, *A Course in Miracles* (Mill Valley, CA: Foundation for Inner Peace, 2007), ACIM, T-20.I.2:5

5. Foundation for Inner Peace, *A Course in Miracles* (Mill Valley, CA: Foundation for Inner Peace, 2007) ACIM, T-16.VII.6:4-6

6. Foundation for Inner Peace, *A Course in Miracles* (Mill Valley, CA: Foundation for Inner Peace, 2007), ACIM, Preface.1:1-3

7. Foundation for Inner Peace, *A Course in Miracles* (Mill Valley, CA: Foundation for Inner Peace, 2007), ACIM, W-202.1:3-5

8. Foundation for Inner Peace, *A Course in Miracles* (Mill Valley, CA: Foundation for Inner Peace, 2007), ACIM, T-16.VI.6:5

9. Foundation for Inner Peace, *A Course in Miracles* (Mill Valley, CA: Foundation for Inner Peace, 2007), ACIM, T-16.VI.8:6

10. Foundation for Inner Peace, *A Course in Miracles* (Mill Valley, CA: Foundation for Inner Peace, 2007), ACIM, T-16.VI.12:1

11. Foundation for Inner Peace, *A Course in Miracles* (Mill Valley, CA: Foundation for Inner Peace, 2007), ACIM, T-28.VII.7:4

14. Foundation for Inner Peace, *A Course in Miracles* (Mill Valley, CA: Foundation for Inner Peace, 2007), ACIM, T-1.I.16:1-2

22. Foundation for Inner Peace, *A Course in Miracles* (Mill Valley, CA: Foundation for Inner Peace, 2007), ACIM, M-14.5:1-6

24. Foundation for Inner Peace, *A Course in Miracles* (Mill Valley, CA: Foundation for Inner Peace, 2007), ACIM, W-119

25. Foundation for Inner Peace, *A Course in Miracles* (Mill Valley, CA: Foundation for Inner Peace, 2007), ACIM, W-119.1:1–2:2

27. Foundation for Inner Peace, *A Course in Miracles* (Mill Valley, CA: Foundation for Inner Peace, 2007), ACIM, W-84.1:1-4

28. Foundation for Inner Peace, *A Course in Miracles* (Mill Valley, CA: Foundation for Inner Peace, 2007), ACIM, T-4.in.2:1-3

30. Foundation for Inner Peace, *A Course in Miracles* (Mill Valley, CA: Foundation for Inner Peace, 2007), ACIM, W-129.3:3

31. Foundation for Inner Peace, *A Course in Miracles* (Mill Valley, CA: Foundation for Inner Peace, 2007), ACIM, W-129.4:1-6

32. Foundation for Inner Peace, *A Course in Miracles* (Mill Valley, CA: Foundation for Inner Peace, 2007), ACIM, W-153.3:1-3

36. Foundation for Inner Peace, *A Course in Miracles* (Mill Valley, CA: Foundation for Inner Peace, 2007), ACIM, T-3.VI.7:4

37. Foundation for Inner Peace, *A Course in Miracles* (Mill Valley, CA: Foundation for Inner Peace, 2007), ACIM, W-84.1:1-4

38. Foundation for Inner Peace, *A Course in Miracles* (Mill Valley, CA: Foundation for Inner Peace, 2007), *ACIM, T-15.XI.10:4-7*

39. Foundation for Inner Peace, *A Course in Miracles* (Mill Valley, CA: Foundation for Inner Peace, 2007), ACIM, T-6.III.3:7

40. Foundation for Inner Peace, *A Course in Miracles* (Mill Valley, CA: Foundation for Inner Peace, 2007), ACIM, T-14.IV.3:4-5

42. Foundation for Inner Peace, *A Course in Miracles* (Mill Valley, CA: Foundation for Inner Peace, 2007), ACIM, T-16.VII.6:4-6

45. Foundation for Inner Peace, *A Course in Miracles* (Mill Valley, CA: Foundation for Inner Peace, 2007), ACIM, T-21.IV.1:3-7

46. Foundation for Inner Peace, *A Course in Miracles* (Mill Valley, CA: Foundation for Inner Peace, 2007), ACIM, T-21.IV.3:1-3

47. Foundation for Inner Peace, *A Course in Miracles* (Mill Valley, CA: Foundation for Inner Peace, 2007), ACIM, T-2.V-A.16:1-6

87. Foundation for Inner Peace, *A Course in Miracles* (Mill Valley, CA: Foundation for Inner Peace, 2007), ACIM, T-26.IV.1:5-7

49. Foundation for Inner Peace, *A Course in Miracles* (Mill Valley, CA: Foundation for Inner Peace, 2007), ACIM, T-14.III.7:5-6

53. Foundation for Inner Peace, *A Course in Miracles* (Mill Valley, CA: Foundation for Inner Peace, 2007), ACIM, W-190.1:1

54. Foundation for Inner Peace, *A Course in Miracles* (Mill Valley, CA: Foundation for Inner Peace, 2007), ACIM, W-137.11:1

56. Foundation for Inner Peace, *A Course in Miracles* (Mill Valley, CA: Foundation for Inner Peace, 2007), ACIM, W-153.1:2-5, ACIM, W-153.2:1-6

58. Foundation for Inner Peace, *A Course in Miracles* (Mill Valley, CA: Foundation for Inner Peace, 2007), ACIM, T-6.III.3:7

63. Foundation for Inner Peace, *A Course in Miracles* (Mill Valley, CA: Foundation for Inner Peace, 2007), ACIM, T-14.IV.6:1-2

64. Foundation for Inner Peace, *A Course in Miracles* (Mill Valley, CA: Foundation for Inner Peace, 2007), ACIM, T-15.XI.10:4-7

66. Foundation for Inner Peace, *A Course in Miracles* (Mill Valley, CA: Foundation for Inner Peace, 2007), ACIM, T-3.IV.1:6

67. Foundation for Inner Peace, *A Course in Miracles* (Mill Valley, CA: Foundation for Inner Peace, 2007), ACIM, W-84.1:1-4

86. Foundation for Inner Peace, *A Course in Miracles* (Mill Valley, CA: Foundation for Inner Peace, 2007), ACIM, W-97.7:2

87. Foundation for Inner Peace, *A Course in Miracles* (Mill Valley, CA: Foundation for Inner Peace, 2007), ACIM, W-201.1:4-6

88. Foundation for Inner Peace, *A Course in Miracles* (Mill Valley, CA: Foundation for Inner Peace, 2007), ACIM, W-pII.14.1:1

89. Foundation for Inner Peace, *A Course in Miracles* (Mill Valley, CA: Foundation for Inner Peace, 2007), ACIM, T-in.2:2-4

90. Foundation for Inner Peace, *A Course in Miracles* (Mill Valley, CA: Foundation for Inner Peace, 2007), ACIM, T-3.IV.2:3

91. Foundation for Inner Peace, *A Course in Miracles* (Mill Valley, CA: Foundation for Inner Peace, 2007), ACIM, T-in.1:6-8

4. Nisargadatta Maharaj, *I Am That* (Durham, NC:1973), *p.6*

12. The Blue Mountain Center for Meditation, *The Bhagavad Gita* (Tomales, CA: 2007), Chapter2

13. Aldous Huxley, *The Perennial Philosophy* (New York, NY: 1945), p14

15. Plato, *The Republic*, (360 B.C.E), Book VII

16. Nisargadatta Maharaj, *I Am That* (Durham, NC:1973), *p.66-67*

17. Nisargadatta Maharaj, *I Am That* (Durham, NC:1973), *p.110*

18. The Blue Mountain Center for Meditation, *The Bhagavad Gita* (Tomales, CA: 2007)

19. The Blue Mountain Center for Meditation, *The Bhagavad Gita* (Tomales, CA: 2007) *The Bhagavad Gita, 2:47-48*

20. The Blue Mountain Center for Meditation, *The Bhagavad Gita* (Tomales, CA: 2007) *The Bhagavad Gita, 2.51*

21. The Blue Mountain Center for Meditation, *The Bhagavad Gita* (Tomales, CA: 2007) *Preface, xxxviii*

23. The Blue Mountain Center for Meditation, *The Bhagavad Gita* (Tomales, CA: 2007)

26. The Blue Mountain Center for Meditation, *The Bhagavad Gita* (Tomales, CA: 2007)

29. Aldous Huxley, *The Perennial Philosophy* (New York, NY: 1945), p24

34. The Blue Mountain Center for Meditation, *The Bhagavad Gita* (Tomales, CA: 2007) https://books.apple.com/us/book/the-bhagavad-gita/id457383796

35. The Blue Mountain Center for Meditation, *The Bhagavad Gita* (Tomales, CA: 2007) https://books.apple.com/us/book/the-bhagavad-gita/id457383796

43. Aldous Huxley, *The Perennial Philosophy* (New York, NY: 1945), The Blue Mountain Center for Meditation, *The Bhagavad Gita* (Tomales, CA: 2007)

51. Dr. Robert O. Young, *Sick and Tired? Reclaim You Inner Terrain,* (CA), https://phmiracleproducts.com/collections/books-audio-video/products/sick-and-tired

52. Dr. Robert O. Young, A Finger on the Magic of Life: Antoine BeChamp - A 19th Century Genius, (CA), https://phmiracleproducts.com/products/a-finger-on-the-magic-of-life-booklet

57. The Blue Mountain Center for Meditation, *The Bhagavad Gita* (Tomales, CA: 2007), 2.5

59. The Blue Mountain Center for Meditation, *The Bhagavad Gita* (Tomales, CA: 2007), 2:371

62. Cynthia Bourgeault, *The Wisdom Jesus*, (Boulder, CO: Shambhala Publications, Inc. 2008), Chapter 8, The Incarnation, p93

Bible Verse

44. Luke 17:20-21 (New Century Version). https://www.biblegateway.com/passage/?search=Luke+17%3A20-21&version=NCV

50. Luke 23:34 (English Standard Version) https://www.biblegateway.com/passage/?search=Luke+23%3A34&version=ESV

65. 2 Peter 1:21 (English Standard Version) https://www.biblegateway.com/verse/en/2%20Peter%201%3A21

70. John 20:17 (English Standard Version) https://www.biblegateway.com/verse/en/John%2020:17

73. John 1:1 (English Standard Version) https://www.biblegateway.com/passage/?search=John+1%3A1&version=CSB

75. Acts 4:10 (English Standard Version) https://www.biblegateway.com/passage/?search=acts+4%3A10&version=ESV

76. Romans 8:11 (English Standard Version) https://www.biblegateway.com/passage/?search=Romans+8%3A11&version=ESV

Article/Blog Post

55. Victor M. Parachin, "Letting Go of Anger—the Buddhist Way," Spirituality & Health (magazine), 2022, https://www.spiritualityhealth.com/letting-go-of-anger-the-buddhist-way

Website

60. Swami Mukundananda, "Bhagavad Gita: Chapter 2, Verse 37," *Holy-Bhagavad-Gita*, 2014, https://www.holy-bhagavad-gita.org/chapter/2/verse/37

61. Alfred Edersheim, "Jesus's Childhood: The Missing Years?," *Christianity*, April 12, 2010, https://www.christianity.com/jesus/life-of-jesus/youth-and-baptism/jesuss-childhood-the-missing-years.html

34. Bhaktivedanta Ashram, "Bhagavad Gita 6.5," *Bhagavad Gita with Commentaries of Ramanuja, Madhva, Shankara and Others*, September 13, 2012 https://www.bhagavad-gita.us/bhagavad-gita-6-5

68. Charles Stanley, "The Roles of the Trinity: Father, Son, and Holy Spirit," *Christianity.com*, 2022, https://www.christianity.com/wiki/god/the-roles-of-the-trinity.html

69. Charles Stanley, "The Roles of the Trinity: Father, Son, and Holy Spirit," *Christianity.com*, 2022, https://www.christianity.com/wiki/god/the-roles-of-the-trinity.html

71. Jack Zavada, "Who Is God the Father Within the Trinity," *LearningReligions.com*, June 2019, https://www.learnreligions.com/god-the-father-701152)

74. Charles Stanley, "The Roles of the Trinity: Father, Son, and Holy Spirit," *Christianity.com*, 2022, https://www.christianity.com/wiki/god/the-roles-of-the-trinity.html

77. Melissa Petruzzello. "Holy Spirit," *Britannica*, May 2023, https://www.britannica.com/topic/Holy-Spirit

78. Mary Fairchild, "Who Is the Holy Spirit," *LearningReligions.com*, May 2019, https://www.learnreligions.com/who-is-the-holy-spirit-701504

79. Merriam-Webster, "Chi," *Merriam-Webster.com*, May 2023, https://www.merriam-webster.com/dictionary/chi

80. Merriam-Webster, "Prana," *Merriam-Webster.com*, June 2023, https://www.merriam-webster.com/dictionary/prana

81. https://www.learnreligions.com/lord-brahma-the-god-of-creation-1770300

82. Merriam-Webster, "Brahma," *Merriam-Webster.com*, May 2023, https://www.merriam-webster.com/dictionary/Brahma

83. Mark Cartwright, "Brahma," *Worldhistory.org*, May 2015, https://www.worldhistory.org/Brahma/

84. Mark Cartwright, "Vishnu," *Worldhistory.org*, Nov 2012, https://www.worldhistory.org/Vishnu/

85. Mark Cartwright, "Shiva," *Worldhistory.org*, May 2018, https://www.worldhistory.org/shiva/

Movie

33. Harold Ramis, dir., *Groundhog Day*, 1993; Woodstock, IL: Columbia Pictures.

41. Lana Wachowski, Lilly Wachowski, dir., *The Matrix,* 1999; Nashville, TN: Warner Brothers.

Printed in the United States
by Baker & Taylor Publisher Services